LIVING FREE
IN AN ANXIOUS WORLD

What Your Doctor and Pastor
Want You to Know About Worry

R. LANNY HUNTER, M.D.
AND VICTOR L. HUNTER, M.DIV., D.MIN.

LEAFWOOD

PUBLISHERS

Abilene, Texas

LIVING FREE IN AN ANXIOUS WORLD
What Your Doctor and Pastor Want You to Know about Worry

LEAFWOOD
P U B L I S H E R S

Copyright 2010 by R. Lanny Hunter and Victor L. Hunter

ISBN 978-0-89112-680-5
LCCN 2010026649

Printed in the United States of America

LIBRARY OF CONGRESS CATALOGING-IN-PUBLICATION DATA
Hunter, R. Lanny.
 Living free in an anxious world : what your doctor and pastor want you to know about worry / R. Lanny Hunter and Victor L. Hunter.
     p. cm.
 ISBN 978-0-89112-680-5
 1. Anxiety--Religious aspects--Christianity. 2. Worry--Religious aspects--Christianity. 3. Peace of mind--Religious aspects--Christianity. 4. Anxiety. 5. Worry. I. Hunter, Victor L., 1942- II. Title.
 BV4908.5.H87 2010
 248.8'6--dc22

                                                                      2010026649

Cover design by Jennette Munger
Interior text design by Sandy Armstrong

Leafwood Publishers is an imprint of
Abilene Christian University Press
1626 Campus Court
Abilene, Texas 79601

1-877-816-4455
www.leafwoodpublishers.com

10 11 12 13 14 15 / 7 6 5 4 3 2 1

LIVING FREE
IN AN ANXIOUS WORLD

Dedication

Ideal teachers are those who use themselves as bridges over
which they invite their students to cross,
then having facilitated their crossing,
joyfully collapse, encouraging them to create bridges of their own.
—Nikos Kazantzakis

To Our Teachers

Mahlon Delp, M.D.
and
Rubem A. Alves, Ph.D.

≥ ≥ ≥

The soul is healed by being with children.
—Fyodor Dostoevsky

And to Our Teachers

Wendy, Lisa, Courtney, Scott
and
Heather, Charisa, Lance

Acknowledgments

This book is dedicated to our teachers.

The first set of teachers, two academics, have had profound influence on our understanding of our disciplines and our vocations.

The second set of teachers, our children, have had profound influence on our lives as human beings.

Both sets of teachers contributed to the "well" from which these insights and reflections have been drawn and we are more grateful to them than our words can express. Included in our gratitude for their companionship in our journey in this anxious world are our wives, Carolyn and Lynette, whose critical insights and proofreading skills have contributed greatly to this book.

We also wish to express thanks to Heidi Nobles (editor) and Leonard Allen (publisher) at Leafwood Publishers for their professional guidance and encouragement in this project.

R. Lanny Hunter and Victor L. Hunter
Season of Pentecost, 2010

Who is in charge of the clattering train? The axles creak and the couplings strain; And the pace is hot, and the points are near, And Sleep has deadened the driver's ear; And the signals flash through the night in vain, For Death is in charge of the clattering train.

—from an 1883 issue of *Punch*

Science without religion is lame.
Religion without science is blind.

—Albert Einstein

Table of Contents

ATTENDING TO ANXIETY

Through the Eyes of a Doctor and Pastor

> "The one therefore who has learned rightly
> to be anxious has learned the most
> important thing."
>
> —Søren Kierkegaard, *The Concept of Dread*

Melanie worried about breast cancer. She had a family history of the disease and had cared for her mother during the terminal phases of her illness. She researched the disease, learning all she could about it. She knew the risk factors. She knew preventive measures. She regularly did a careful self-examination. She discussed her concerns with her physician. She had the appropriately scheduled mammograms.

The morning she discovered the small lump in her left breast, her adrenalin shot sky high. She immediately called her physician for an appointment. Diagnosis was prompt and treatment begun in the early stages of her illness. Today Melanie is doing fine, participates in a support group of breast cancer survivors, and continues a regimen of self-care.

When Melanie was diagnosed she said to her doctor, "I was afraid of that." Melanie's fear was both appropriate and life-saving. She engaged in "good worry," enabling her to become proactive. She did not simply "stew" about her fear, nor did she deny it by playing the role of the ostrich. She used her worry positively in order to address the negative. She exercised careful loving attention, the very essence of good worry and wise self-care.

Theoretical and practical studies of anxiety have been conducted for decades, perhaps centuries, depending on one's definitions of "theoretical," "practical," and "anxiety." These studies have come from numerous disciplines: theology, philosophy, psychology, psychiatry, sociology, general medicine, anthropology, anatomy, biochemistry, literature, and the arts. Observations on anxiety have ranged from the sublime—Dostoyevsky's *The Brothers Karamazov*—to the ridiculous—*Mad Magazine*'s Alfred E. Newman and his *non sequitur*, "What, me worry?!" From "bootstrap advice"—*The Power of Positive Thinking*—to delusional religion—"Name It and Claim It." From bogus science to PET scans of the living, functioning brain. And throughout, victims of anxiety have soldiered on with attitudes ranging from clenched-teeth defiance to a scorched earth gratitude for the tutorial of anxiety.

Bringing Together Medicine and Theology

This book is written from the perspective of our two disciplines (medicine and theology) and our two professions (physician and pastor). It draws on years of schooling, reflection, reading, more than eighty years of clinical and pastoral experiences, and approximately one hundred and thirty years in the trenches of life. We feel acutely the inadequacy of that knowledge base, since all knowledge must be grasped with a humble hand.

This book also draws on the long Christian tradition and our own experience of faith. We make no apologies for our Christian faith. We believe whole persons need personal, vocational, social, recreational, artistic, and religious dimensions to life. If references to faith are off-putting, this book is probably not for you. We suggest, however, that everyone does have a philosophical dimension to their lives. It may be centered in creeds based upon hedonism, rationalism, intellectualism, barbarism, atheism, scientism, naturalism, materialism, polytheism, Republicanism, capitalism, fascism, Marxism, Buddhism, or any other *ism*. A philosophy doesn't have to use God-talk to be a religion. Nor does it have to have a religious perspective to be embraced with a narrow-minded literal fanaticism. Any philosophy or myth to which we give our allegiance and by which we order our lives is a religion. Every religion is a choice, a leap of faith. The religion to which we bow down must be big enough to hold within its power our personal story, must address the larger questions about life and living, and must have a reasonable shelf on which to place those questions that are ambiguous, paradoxical, or unanswerable. The authors of this book have chosen the Christian religion as our creedal, philosophical, mythical choice around which we attempt to order our lives. Faith always carries within its core a kernel of doubt, and it certainly does for us. But that is where we take our stand. Read along with us as we address the questions of worry and anxiety from the perspective of our two disciplines and the tradition and experience of our faith.

A Word about Language

In writing about science and theology, we will try to avoid technical and academic language. Such language is drawn from long historical, cultural, and practical usage, and is valuable because a single word can replace a paragraph of explanation and description. This allows practitioners of every vocation to use its own special language to communicate efficiently and accurately. This is true for farmers, automobile mechanics, firefighters, computer experts, stock brokers, lawyers, and ice cream vendors. However, such language usually closes the door on the person who is not initiated into the special secrets of that discipline. Nowhere is this truer than for medical doctors and theologians, whose technical language is often rooted in Hebrew, Latin, and Greek. This sometimes makes our fields seem not only inaccessible, but somehow snobbish. We hope to avoid these linguistic stumbling blocks by keeping the material here simple and straightforward, and by providing accessible definitions when necessary.

A Word about Experts

We want to say a word about experts. There is an "equal and opposite" expert for every theme and topic, whether we're considering history, science, religion, philosophy, war, or politics. This is evidenced in every courtroom where the experts line up and swear to "tell the truth, the whole truth, and nothing but the truth," and proceed to express their expert and opposite views for both the prosecution and defense. There is a certain silly aggravation in such contradiction, but its strength lies in keeping all discussions open in an enlightened search for understanding. The challenge for all of us, and in all situations, is to be discriminating thinkers and talkers. In a time when language is systematically abused and emptied of meaning, we must cultivate a serious skepticism for expert pronouncements. It follows that there is good and bad science, good and bad religion, good and bad aeronautics, good and bad medicine, good and bad diets, and good and bad philosophy. We cannot descend into spineless relativism where every notion that comes down the pike is regarded to be of equal worth. There really are good and bad ideas. We are responsible for evaluating "expert" opinions and making decisions.

Goals and Parameters

In this small book, we intend to take a serious look at anxiety, recognizing that we cannot be comprehensive. We will take a look at the medical and pathological aspects of anxiety from various scientific disciplines, knowing that we cannot be exhaustive. We will address the religious issues raised by anxiety, fully aware that we cannot offer a comprehensive theology of anxiety. Our aims are modest but serious. From our disciplines of science and theology and our professions of doctor and pastor, we hope to offer insights, education, and encouragement in facing the dangers and challenges of being human. We will consider genuine threats and perceived threats to our well-being. We will address worries that stalk us because we know we are mortal. Most of us fear death. We will attempt to pursue a deeper understanding of our humanity, where faith, hope, and love coalesce into the prospect of a fulfilling life—a life in which, despite the threats we face from loss and alienation, purpose, joyful relationships, and freedom become possibilities.

We believe that the road of freedom through the landscape of anxiety opens only to those who find the courage, in a worried world and an anxious age, to seize the moment, take the initial steps, say "Thank God," and keep putting one foot in front of the other. In the physician's language, we say we are recovering from disease. In the pastor's language, we turn to Isaiah and say with the prophet that sometimes we can "mount up with wings like eagles," sometimes we can "run and not grow weary," and at other times it is all we can do to "walk and not faint." Destructive worry fragments our lives. Whether we seek healing from physical disease or spiritual suffering, we are making an effort to find wholeness.

Wholeness is not perfection, but a state of living life whole—realistically, constructively, and completely.

Chapter One

HUMAN LIMITATIONS AND COSMIC LAMENTATIONS

People are Worriers

"The human state: inconstancy, boredom, anxiety."

—Blaise Paschal, *Pensées*

Gary worried all the time. Literally. He worried about his job, he worried about his finances, he worried about his health. He worried about his wife and his children. He worried about the future. He worried when things were going badly. He worried even more when things seemed to be going well. He worried about death. There wasn't a moment of peace in the midst of pervasive, uncontainable fretfulness. His mind buzzed with worry like a gnat's incessant pestering of a drop of sweat on a fluttering eyelid, circling around the same things again and again. As his mind chewed on worry, worry chewed on him . . . muscle tension, occasional "shakes" and diarrhea. His experience with constant and uncontrollable worry had gone on for months. He couldn't sleep well and was increasingly irritable with his family and colleagues. He even worried about worry and couldn't identify or nail down his concerns. They were simply like gas filling a room. And when one worry would let up, another was waiting in the wings to take its place. He was chronically fatigued. He became the "poor player that struts and frets his hour upon the stage" . . . only the hour was never-ending. Recently he had begun to dread the arrival of the mail and was unable to open his letters or his bills. He feared they contained bad news or some threatening situation. Finally, with the support and encouragement of his wife, he went to see his pastor.

Gary was one of the six and a half million Americans who suffer from general anxiety disorder (GAD) every year. His heightened and ever-present sense of worry infected not only his own peace of mind, but also his family's sense of well-being. He could no longer engage life and work in a consistently constructive or positive way. GAD is an expression of being "worried sick."

People are worriers. That about sums it up. Anxiety is a fact of life. It's so common as to be natural. And, there are good reasons why we worry. There is plenty to worry about! This fact may be unsettling to those who embrace the Christian faith. After all, in his Sermon on the Mount, Jesus told his audience that kingdom people needn't worry about things like clothing and food. He used a metaphor of lilies and birds to illustrate that flora and fauna didn't worry and still, respectively, they are fed daily and richly attired. Jesus assured his listeners that a kingdom person is much more valuable to the Father than lilies and birds, and that they, too, would be taken care of every day of their lives. Yes, death awaits us all. But then, the apostle Paul tells us that the victory over death is already won through Jesus. Aren't these sufficient grace notes for us?

Well, yes, as Christians we believe that. But in reality, many of us hold those convictions with a frail hand, like Thomas, the doubter. In our humanity, we are still afflicted with assorted worries—and we can't overcome things we won't face. It is necessary for us to acknowledge legitimate realities that unsettle us. So take a deep breath; we're going to face the worst for a few pages so we can find our way clear to more hopeful living.

Death. We might as well begin with the end. The precariousness of life and the certainty of death is a reality with which we all live. This makes life worrisome and existence anxious.

Health. Here today, gone tomorrow. There is no place to hide when our bodies betray us.

Social Relationships. Broken ties, broken vows, broken marriages, broken families, broken friendships. Isolation and alienation. Disconnectedness. Trust gone bad. Constant separation anxiety.

Aging Parents and Vulnerable Children. No one is safe. Diminishment and danger stalk the people we love.

Economics. Job security is tenuous. Social "security" is threatened. Retirement with a pension is uncertain. Economic difficulty if not disaster is a month's paycheck away for most people. Money makes us crazy, whether we have it or don't!

Change. The rapid pace of change in all areas of life threatens us with a tidal wave of uncertainty. Changing roles, changing expectations, changing values. Changing technologies, changing meanings, changing cultural foundations. Changing communities and changing times. Are there any continuities and connections left?

Self-doubt. Each day is filled with competition (even for children at an ever-earlier age). I am faced constantly with challenges and choices. Am I up to it? Am I good enough, talented enough, beautiful enough, tough enough, strong enough? Am I smart enough? Am I worthy? Will people like me, think I am an oaf, make fun of me, or simply ignore me? In parenting, at work, in life . . . the possibility of failure lurks everywhere.

Suffering. Suffering can be found on every street, in all communities, at any address, within any body, and on any mind. It is a pervasive, unavoidable, and constant fact of life.

Evil. Evil is on the prowl, and its foreboding shadow falls across even the sunlit landscape of our lives. Terrible things happen, and they happen to all people at some time. It is as if a malevolent ghost haunts the universe. Life is not safe, trustworthy, or certain.

Destiny. What is the meaning and purpose of my life? Do I count for anything at all? Is there a God? If so, what does that mean? Is there a judgment? What about heaven and hell? Am I saved? Will I be saved? How do I deal with my doubts, my fears, my uncertainties, and my confusions?

From the Personal to the Social and Cosmic

That short list of very real, ever-present, everyday worries includes very personal experiences, but it also has social, even cosmic, dimensions. There is a nationwide tuberculosis epidemic with a germ that is resistant to current antibiotics. AIDS is a scourge that affects people across all genders, ages, and social classes of the global population. It can be contracted by being a Good Samaritan and helping a bleeding accident victim who is, though you don't know it, HIV positive. Every few months some virus—like the Avian Flu virus—mutates and threatens to become a pestilential plague.

The world is at each other's throats, and the split between the Middle Eastern and Western societies is the most divisive it has been since the Crusades. Our own country either has or suggests it will tear up international agreements from trade treaties to the Geneva Convention. Violent crime now spills over into every town and neighborhood. The entire world is divided into the haves and have-nots. The wealthy individuals and the wealthy nations either can't or won't do what it takes to correct injustice and provide the basics of life for their own people, let alone people of other nations.

Is global warming real or just junk science? How interconnected are our ecosystems and economies? We have polluted land, polluted air, and polluted rivers, lakes, and oceans. There is a crisis of energy as the world uses up fossil fuels. There is over-population and over-crowding. There are bloated people, bloated budgets, and bloated bureaucracies. Not just jobs, but whole companies and entire industries are outsourced to nations where labor is plentiful and cheap.

The despotic, ruthless nations are an entirely different matter. They often have no interest in their own poor and needy and even exploit them for political advantage. This creates a climate in which the have-nots believe it is necessary to take what they need from the people and nations who have it. Terrorism is loosed upon the world, whether in the form of suicidal/homicidal bombers with improvised explosive devices or trained armies with sophisticated weapons. And the situation is only intensified when perpetrators of violence tie their actions to religion. Is there a God? Whose God is it? Well, *my* God! What I think is what He/She thinks, and you'd better believe it! Nothing is more vicious than war waged in the name of a deity—any deity will do.

And then, we always come back to the ever-present, over-arching shadow of death. Death waits insidiously in every automobile accident, murderous thought, contemplated mayhem, and terrifying fury of nature. Death lurks in your kindly doctor's mistakes, your country lawyer's mendacity, a developer's greed, a CEO's arrogance, a fraudulent marketing claim, an Internet scam, and in the industrial pollutants leached into society, either knowingly, carelessly, or ignorantly.

Yes, there's plenty to worry about. Anxiety is a healthy response to threats to our well-being; properly channeled, our fears help us overcome adversity and thrive in our environments.

Worry and Biology

Aside from all of the very real personal, global, and cosmic worries that rightly nag at us, there is also a basic biological reason that we worry. One basic emotion that is hardwired throughout the animal kingdom—including the human species—is fear. Of course, we can also experience a range of many other emotions—contentment, joy, ecstasy, love, loyalty, anger, jealousy, peevishness, hatred—all arising out of a very complex, highly developed brain that is hooked up to the entire body. But frankly, the biology and chemistry of our bodies don't really care whether we are happy.

Happiness isn't essential to life. Human nature cares about this pleasant emotion, and we stretch ourselves to attain it. This striving is one of the things that make us human—we possess the capacity to be more than our biology and chemistry. But fear, because it is essential for survival, is an instinct that is simple, lightning-fast, and hard as nails.

Fear begins in a little nub of nerve tissue located deep within the brain called the amygdala. The name itself even sounds ominous and sinister. The amygdala is about the size and shape of an almond (hence its name, Latin for almond). It perches at the top of the spinal cord and contains clumps of nerves and cells simmered in a chemical broth. The amygdala lurks in the brain of every creature alive today. It is chained lightning, crackling with energy, and waiting to strike in fear and rage. Its fundamental purpose is to protect the creature from danger. Fight-or-flight. This reflex arcs out of the amygdala to activate the entire biological apparatus—heart, lungs, bowel, blood vessels, muscles, adrenal glands, eyes, and ears.

The amygdala is on red alert twenty-four hours a day, seven days a week, and three hundred and sixty-five days a year, ready to sound the alarm. The entire human organism in all of its complexity is caught up in this. The reflex arcs of the nervous system. The hormones of the endocrine system. The pumps and pressure gauges of the cardiovascular system. The emergency fuel system of the muscle groups. The enzymes and neurotransmitters of biochemistry. The human receptors of eye, ear, nose, taste, and touch.

Perhaps twenty-first-century humans don't need this crash-cart system for survival as much as our cave-dwelling ancestors did, but we have it, nonetheless. It is still part and parcel of our survival. There are no saber-toothed tigers stalking us, but the system is still absolutely vital for climbing ladders, hiking a steep mountain trail, moving through underbrush in rattlesnake country, lighting the charcoal in our BBQ, carving the Thanksgiving turkey with a razor-sharp knife, hunting out the odd sound downstairs in the dead of night, driving a car, or walking a lonely, dark street in the city. And that's just for those of us with relatively noncombative jobs—the fear/fight/flight response is critical for personnel working in the areas of animal control, law enforcement, fire fighting, military service, and search-and-rescue.

Fear is primal. Hunger and sexual desire also appear in the surface level of instincts in the descending hierarchy of human emotion. All other emotions—love, jealousy, hatred, sorrow, happiness, and the myriad remaining more nuanced emotions—are secondary. Humankind's glory and diversity is grounded in its capacity to experience these secondary emotions, some of which are learned, because they sweeten the human experience. They also make it both bitter and bittersweet. These complex emotions have created human culture from the hearth to the Holocaust. They are responsible for poetry and entice us to reach for the stars. But fear is the primeval, instinctual, bedrock emotion at the base of human experience. Fear programmed humans to fight or flee, a very necessary adaptation for survival. Human beings, then, have a natural tendency to be afraid. Fear is good! And so is worry, the first corollary to fear. The goal, therefore, is not to stamp out worry, but to learn how to respond to it.

In evolutionary terms, the fearful creatures that adapted a "smart" worrying process not only survived but prospered, while those creatures who failed to worry smart died out. But instincts can go awry. The adaptive process can become maladapted, warped, and twisted. Worry is good only up to a point. Modern people have taken the body's primitive response to physical danger (fight-or-flight) and attached it to not just real physical danger, but *perceived* danger. The perceived danger that prompts fight-or-flight may be physical, psychological, social, or spiritual, but it touches off the same explosive cascade of instincts as physical danger. Just as the soldier in combat has a constant, chronic biological response to fear, the worrier has the same constant, chronic biological response to worry. For both soldier and worrywart, the biological response endures beyond the moment of immediate threat. For both, the feelings and biological responses initially triggered by fear and worry morph into a long, low-grade sense of impending calamity. Worry, thus maladapted, becomes a malady, or a sickness.

Our goal is not to avoid worry, but to worry constructively rather than destructively. Constructive, "smart" worry makes us aware of real danger or a genuine problem and allows us to takes steps to prepare and hopefully prevent a bad outcome. Destructive worry is "foolish worry" that sees—even seeks—unsolvable problems that deteriorate into innumerable possible disasters.

In this book, we want to consider how we can be both scientist and philosopher with our worry. When worry confronts us, we must grasp it with both hands, look it squarely in the eye, scrutinize it, analyze it, dissect it, dice it into its component parts, and evaluate them. They must be named, measured, and weighed. Then we are on the way to changing destructive worry into constructive worry.

Chapter Two

CULTURAL DIAGNOSIS AND CLARIFYING DEFINITIONS

Voices from an Anxious World

"A crust eaten in peace is better than a
banquet partaken in anxiety."

—Aesop, "The Town Mouse and the Country Mouse"

Susan, a highly competent executive secretary with major responsibilities in a successful corporation, woke from a deep sleep with a start. Her husband stirred next to her, turned over, and continued sleeping. She was terrified. She couldn't catch her breath, feeling as if she was choking. Her heart was pounding, and she was wet with sweat. Yet she was not in pain, thinking initially she might be having a heart attack. A terrible sense of foreboding overtook her. She felt she was about to die.

She sat up but couldn't get comfortable. She lay back down, but it was more difficult to breathe. She got out of bed, highly agitated, and walked around the house, finally going outside on the back porch. "I must be losing my mind," she thought. Slowly, the feeling subsided. "What is wrong with me?" She realized these "attacks" were becoming more frequent and were occurring at different times during the day and night, unrelated to any stimuli. At night, they were disturbing her sleep, filling her with fear and apprehension. During the day, she would suddenly feel the need to escape the "nerves." But she couldn't escape, run away, or hide from her body. Her shortness of breath was inside her, and her anxiety was palpable. The episodes were beginning to affect her sense of well-being, her sleep patterns, her social relationships, and her work habits. And she couldn't control them.

Susan was suffering from a panic attack, identified in the psychiatric literature in the categories of both "mood disorders" and "anxiety disorders." Panic attacks that are recurring and intense need to be attended to professionally. They can disrupt life, social relationships, and work, robbing the sufferer of any sense of peace of mind or security. They are a manifestation of one of the ways we can become "worried sick."

Worry is like a great river meandering though the landscape of our lives. It's shallow enough for the child to wade in. It's deep enough for the adult to swim in. When the River Worry stays within its banks, it sustains life. It quenches thirst, washes us clean, and waters abundant gardens and crops. It irrigates pleasant pastures and provides intellectual, emotional, and physical bounty. The River Worry is a moat to shield and protect us, and a provocative channel that stimulates our imagination. When it overflows its banks, its churning flood waters engulf us and strip away security, peace, and joy. The person who gets caught up in its most threatening swirling currents can be drowned and carried out to sea.

Sophocles believed the work of poets and writers is to "see life steady and to see it whole." This is also the work of doctors and pastors—the work of the healing arts and sciences and of theology, philosophy, and religion. Our goal is to discuss worry and anxiety and understand its blessings and cursings. As we discussed in chapter one, helpful worry averts trouble and disaster, while toxic worry (an affliction that troubles millions) creates disease, and sometimes a living hell. Viewed from the particular disciplines of medicine and theology, worry and anxiety are not philosophical abstractions, but powerful forces that are part of the human condition and manifest themselves on a daily basis. We will attempt to "see them steadily and to see them whole" as they are experienced in the actual cut and thrust of living—as we all live and work, suffer and play, remember and hope—in both our lonely solitude and in our communal lives.

Voices Addressing Anxiety

We must begin by examining Western culture at the beginning of the twenty-first century. There is perhaps no better way to do this than to listen to voices of the poet, the novelist, the humorist, the psychotherapist, the theologian, the philosopher, the ethicist, and the psychiatrist/psychologist.

The Poet: W. H. Auden

"Muster no monsters, I'll meeken my own." So wrote W. H. Auden in 1950 in his epic poem, "The Age of Anxiety." Anxiety is Auden's diagnosis of the cultural emotion rampant in the last half of the twentieth century. People young and old are filled with anxiety because anxiety belongs to the very nature of being human. Auden writes that we need to "go away with our terrors until we have taught them to sing." The characters in Auden' s poem must deal with the experiences of loneliness and alienation, the dissolution of the culture of modernism, the loss of certitudes, the weakening of values, the inability to suffer redemptively, the failure of courage to love or be loved, the disappearance of meaningful community, and the dwindling of meaning and meaningful communication. Anxiety imprisons both our imaginations and our actions. Anxiety cuts us off from a fulfilled and meaningful life. And yet, the very nature of anxiety and worry is to subvert the courage and creativity it takes to deal with it. Auden writes:

> Yet the noble despair of poets
> is nothing of the sort; it is silly
> to refuse the tasks of time.

Auden here expresses that to see life steadily and to see it whole is to recognize the monster of anxiety and then move forward from paralyzing fear to actions that engage life.

The Novelist: Albert Camus

Among the many novelists who deal with the issue of anxiety in our time and culture, Albert Camus stands out. His description of this past century as "the century of fear" is unrelenting in his fiction. His characters are haunted by a free-floating anxiety in which they recognize their vulnerability and struggle to establish values and act in ways that overcome the limitations and terrors of being human. Camus explores the human hunger for love and freedom that are essential to confronting the monster of anxiety and being fully human. The dilemma of our human quest is that we must engage life while being aware of life's underlying absurdity.

In his fiction, Camus confronts us with the question of fear in our anxious lives, the hunger for love and community in the face of our anxiety, the desire for freedom from bondage, and the search for meaning when faced with absurdity. Fear before the vicissitudes of life has been used to account for humankind's need for religion.

However, the exact opposite may be true. As David E. Roberts writes in his 1955 book, *The Grandeur and Misery of Man*, "Our age, having dispensed almost entirely with fear of God, now finds itself paralyzed with dread when it contemplates man and his powers. What makes this dread so acute is loss of faith—the sense that civilization has gone empty at the core." This cosmic view is easily personalized in the lives of individuals. Anxiety, worry, and fear manifest themselves in the feeling that our own lives are empty at the core.

The Humorists: Alfred E. Newman and Woody Allen

Alfred E. Newman, the Everyman of *Mad Magazine*, is best remembered for his *non sequitur* "What, me worry?" We laugh as he denies his anxiety in the very act of expressing his fear. The role of the clown in our culture is to wear the sad face in the midst of laughter and the happy face in the midst of absurdity. The clown makes us laugh at what we think about and to think about what we laugh about. Humor is often found in that which hurts us, terrifies us, and leaves us feeling most vulnerable. Like worry and fear, humor and pain are twins. "What, me worry?" You'd better believe it.

That we are a worried people has also been portrayed in the films of Woody Allen—the Everyman of fidgety fearfulness. *Manhattan*, a 1979 MGM award-winning romantic comedy (which Allen wrote, directed, and starred in) has a classic scene that captures the worried man. The male lead, Allen himself, all twitchy and sweaty, has gone to see his best friend, who teaches at Columbia University. The conversation takes place in a science lab against the incongruous backdrop of three human skeletons and one prehistoric skeleton. The scene ends with a close-up of Allen standing beside the pre-historic skeleton, nattering on about human frailties, broken relationships, and sexuality. Allen's character is in one of the world's great cities, in the science lab of one of the world's great universities, a fully-fleshed, sentient man of the twentieth century who is paralyzed by anxiety and despair, carrying on alongside his gawping ancestor who is the quintessential image of death. This juxtaposition is a moment of brilliant cinema, at once uproariously funny and tragically pathetic.

The Psychotherapist: Rollo May

Rollo May, the existential psychotherapist, published *The Meaning of Anxiety* in 1950. He emphasized anxiety as the epicenter of all human experience and formulated theories of anxiety that encompass culture, history, psychology, and biology. May believes that anxiety runs much deeper than peripheral threats to our well-being. He writes that anxiety "arises from the fact that the values and standards underlying modern culture are themselves threatened."

In the Western world, from the first century to the twentieth century, people generally accepted that God provided the answers to our human predicament. These answers were universal—they applied to everyone, everywhere, all the time. This understanding was a guiding light. With the rise of science, Western civilization accepted that physical data provided the key to our human predicament. These answers were also universal and applied to everyone, everywhere, all the time. This new guiding light was termed "modernism." We now live in a world where a significant segment of humankind believes that proffered answers to the human predicament are not universal and do not apply to everyone, everywhere, all the time. This perspective is termed "postmodernism" and operates on the conviction that all answers are local and limited. There are no common, accepted cultural values by which we can communicate, find meaning, and form community. In such a setting, it might be argued that one idea is as good as any other. The underlying assumptions of the culture itself are threatened. It is difficult to find a secure place to stand.

Postmodernism often has two results. First, we may succumb to anyone with the loud voice of absolutism. We embrace fanaticism because it seems to offer irrefutable, unassailable ground. Second, we may become useless, gutted of conviction with nothing to offer anyone, anywhere or anytime. Relativism rules! There is no common ground and no solid ground. Society has erected a new Tower of Babel, and we have become the "chattering classes." There is psychobabble, religious babble, political babble, scientific babble, cultural babble, fanatical babble, and timorous babble.

The threat to postmodern people is that anxiety is not only an external threat—war, famine, death, and disease—but an internal one. The cultural ground is shifting, and we can't get a foothold on the undulating path. The foundations of our house have turned to sand.

The Theologian: Paul Tillich

One of the major "theologians of anxiety" of the twentieth century was Paul Tillich. He argued that anxiety is simply a reality, something that belongs to human existence itself. As part of human existence, the elimination of anxiety in human life is not a proper goal. The basis of anxiety in the human creature as a finite being is the very threat that is part of human existence. Since this is so, eliminating anxiety from human experience is neither a realistic nor a proper goal. The basis of anxiety is that human beings know themselves to be finite (small and limited) and vulnerable (we will all die). We know that death is not only inevitable, it is also not local. It is universal. This is a shattering fact for the postmodern world—the grave is what happens to everyone, everywhere, all the time. Death is truly the end of everything. There is no afterlife, no heaven, no hell. There is just an all-encompassing, comprehensive nothingness. However, this nothingness belongs not just to the cessation of life. It is manifested in life in the threat of meaninglessness. Thus the threat of non-being threatens the very existence of the self.

Tillich believed this threat is the source of human anxiety. Much of his theological work was devoted to helping us find the courage to live in the face of ultimate nothingness. For him, facing this anxiety was a religious question, and he focused his theology on questions surrounding the meaning of our existence. He centered his concerns on "being human" in relation to "being itself"— the overcoming of the threat of non-being.

The Philosopher: Soren Kierkegaard

Soren Kierkegaard, the Danish philosopher of the nineteenth century, laid the foundations for twentieth-century existential thought. Existential is a word that stops us dead in our tracks. It simply stumps us.

Existentialism, simply put, is concerned with the uniqueness of human existence and individual human experience. What does it mean to be a free and responsible human being (a self) in a universe that is indifferent to us? Every moment of our life is filled with the choice to actually live or to turn away from life. Choosing to actually live depends on whether we can confront anxiety and then make the choice to engage life in each moment. Anxiety can deform and deny living freely. It can become a "sickness unto death" in Kierkegaard's terms, defeating our choice to genuinely live each moment of existence.

The existentialist believes that life in each moment is filled with potential, and that there are numerous possibilities for fulfillment. These possibilities must be identified and then freely chosen. The human capacity to choose freely fills us with anxiety because we know we might fail. If anxiety prevents us from freely choosing and moving successively from moment to moment with life's opportunities, our present is diminished and our future fades into the distance. We lose hope. We are paralyzed. Kierkegaard wrote, "In the eyes of the world it is dangerous to venture. And why? Because one may lose. But not to venture is shrewd." And yet by not venturing, we lose that which it would be difficult to lose in even the most "venturesome venture"—one's self. "If I have ventured amiss—very well," Kierkegaard said in *Sickness Unto Death* (as translated by Walter Lowrie in 1941), "then life helps me by its punishment. But if I have not ventured at all—who then helps me?" Unless we confront anxiety and attend to worry, our lives are reduced to fear, immobility, and stagnation. The fear of failure in the face of anxiety *is* failure. Life is denied. We transpose "nothing ventured, nothing gained" into "nothing tried, nothing lost." But we *do* lose. We lose our humanity with its potential for a full life.

The Ethicist: Reinhold Niebuhr

Reinhold Niebuhr adds his considerable voice to the chorus of people who believe anxiety is at the center of human nature. To be human is to be anxious. We are marked at birth for worry. But Niebuhr argues that while we suffer all the limitations of our biology and our human nature, we also have the ability (because we are mind and spirit, too) to reflect on our circumstances and rise above them through conscious choice and acts of free will. The inner conflict inherent in this tension manifests itself in anxiety. Niebuhr's beliefs underlie his famous prayer, a part of which became the prayer of Alcoholics Anonymous: "God, give us the grace to accept with serenity the things that cannot be changed, the courage to change the things that should be changed, and the wisdom to distinguish the one from the other."

It is important to note that when we speak (or Niebuhr speaks) of the human body with its "limitations," we are not denigrating the body as something inferior to the mind/spirit in some kind of Greek dualistic understanding of our humanity. We are not saying "body is bad" and "spirit is good." We are affirming a holistic understanding of *persons* in God's good creation (in the Hebrew sense), not some bifurcated being "made up" of part physical body and part spiritual soul, a sort of Dr. Jekyll and Mr. Hyde manifestation of bad body/good spirit. As John A. T. Robinson writes, the human being does not "have a body, he is a body, the whole conceived as a psycho-physical unity." Instead, it is important to recognize that in our very wholeness as human persons, we live in a complex of both limitations and possibilities, determinisms and freedoms.

The Psychiatrist and the Psychologist: Sigmund Freud and Karen Horney

The psychiatric literature of the past century is filled with references to the role anxiety plays in mental and emotional disorders. There is a difference between anxiety and anxiety disorders, and we will turn our attention to pathological anxiety in a later chapter. For now, it is important simply to add the voice of this discipline to the diagnosis of our Western culture.

Sigmund Freud believed that anxiety is the single, central problem leading to emotional and behavioral disorders. Karen Horney diagnosed anxiety as the dynamic center of neurosis. The psychoanalytic tradition has focused on attending to the phenomenon of neurosis. Neurotic anxiety, which lies at the heart of this phenomenon, blocks us from a fulfilled and joyful life because it limits our actions, increases our fears, reduces our energies, and keeps us from moving forward toward our goals. It blocks our growth as human beings by short-circuiting our thinking, our feelings, and our actions. The ability to realize our potential as whole persons is stymied.

The Culture of Stress, Anxiety, and Worry

All these witnesses of our culture—the poet, the novelist, the humorists, the psychotherapist, the theologian, the philosopher, the ethicist, the psychiatrist, and the psychologist—indicate that the cultural home we have inherited at the beginning of this millennium is a haunted house. It is haunted by anxiety, worry, and stress.

Some of these ghosts can be named. Some are elusive apparitions. They can multiply in number and power until they take over.

Lewis Thomas, physician and writer, observed of humans, "We are, perhaps, uniquely among the earth's creatures, the worrying animal. We worry away our lives, fearing the future, discontent with the present, unable to take in the idea of dying, unable to sit still." Edmund Bourne and Lorna Garano point out that three things contribute to the prevalence of pathological anxiety in our culture. First, the pace at which we live our lives, including the pace of technological development, contributes to our stress. Second, our culture lacks any consensus about standards and values. Third, we live at a time of increased social alienation, when we are disconnected from God, family, friends, and any genuine experience of community.

Epidemiologists and statisticians—the number crunchers—support these conclusions. A recent survey of primary care physicians in the United States revealed that at least one-third of office visits were prompted by some form of anxiety. Over the course of a lifetime, one in four people will suffer from medical conditions called anxiety disorders. This means sixty-five million Americans are suffering from anxiety disorders, and many millions more suffer from sub-clinical problems such as tension, worry, stress, low self-esteem, and the blahs. In a January 1999 bulletin, the National Institute of Mental Health declared that anxiety disorders are the most common mental health problem in America. Anxiety costs our economy a total of forty-six billion dollars, including thirty-four billion dollars in lost productivity. To provide a sense of what these statistics mean, let us cite the old television show *The Naked City*, a show that followed the life of one person in New York City each week. The show ended with this voice-over: "There are eight million stories in the naked city. This has been one of them." What might accurately be added to such a voice-over is this: "Of the eight million stories in New York City, more than two million are about anxiety and anxiety disorders."

Definitions and Images

Surveys and statistics are interesting for bringing to light the overwhelming prevalence of the situation, but our real concern is the people who cannot deal with the normal experience of anxiety. Their lives are painful and limited by abnormal anxiety. Our goal is to help those who desire to overcome their anxiety, fear of failure, fear of social embarrassment, their fear of life, and ultimately their fear of death. Before doing so, we want to try to define worry and anxiety in working terms for readers.

We should first note that worry and anxiety are flip sides of the same coin; for all practical purposes, no distinction need be made. If there is a distinction it is probably one of degree. We can say that *worry* is mental distress. Worry is unremitting agitation. Worry is obsessive fear of threats (real or imagined) to one's well-being. The mind is bogged down in unending uncertainty. Worry disquiets the mind and exhausts the body. We might say that *anxiety* is painful apprehension over an impending or anticipated problem or disaster. Anxiety causes mental stress and physical illness. The body sweats, the blood pressure goes up, the stomach pumps out increased digestive acid, and the muscles tense. Doubt and defeatism take over. These definitions and descriptions easily get bogged down in wordiness. Interestingly, when we turn to Webster's New Collegiate Dictionary, we find that the word comes down to us from an old High German word, *wurgen*. *Wurgen* means to strangle or to choke. This picture is worth a thousand words. Worry strangles or chokes us, and it may even choke us to death.

Robert Gerzon, using powerful word pictures of his own, depicted our goals when confronted with worry and anxiety. He said we must learn to ride the dragon of natural anxiety, confront the monster of toxic anxiety, and wrestle with the angel of sacred anxiety. If we are able to do this successfully, we won't strangle on life. We may even find healing and hope, love and community, courage and freedom.

Chapter Three

THE SCIENCE OF WORRY AND ANXIETY

What's Distinctive about Humans?

"The basic anxiety, the anxiety of a finite being about the threat of non-being, cannot be eliminated. It belongs to existence itself."

—Paul Tillich, *The Courage To Be*

Elizabeth's hectic lifestyle was wearing her out. She was a working mom, with a girl in pre-school and a boy in the second grade. Her husband—struggling at an entry level position in a large, urban law firm—helped with the kids, but at their age, they turned to her for much of their care and support. In any case, her husband faced his own set of problems in a cut-throat job that required a fixed number of billable hours per month. Between the kids, her husband, and her position at the advertising agency, there was never enough time. Elizabeth worried about being there for her kids and wished she could stop working, at least for a while, but even their modest lifestyle required two incomes. Yet she fretted that she didn't have enough time and energy to compete with the men in her agency for the top accounts and the steady promotions. For the past three weeks, she had been working on a presentation, and it had been a constant worry. Moreover, the day of the presentation, she was especially nervous. She was sweating and her heart pounded so much that she thought it would jump out of her chest. She was mortified to find that her hands shook at a critical time in her speech. That night, her husband wanted to make love, but she was just too agitated to be there for him. She felt terrible. Exhausted, she still had difficulty sleeping.

The only good thing that had happened during the last few months, Elizabeth reflected, was her weight loss. She tended to pudginess and had always found it difficult to maintain her ideal weight. It had been especially difficult to shed the unwanted pounds gained during two pregnancies. But over the past few months, eleven pounds had simply melted away. She hadn't looked so good since college. All she needed was some medicine for her nerves and a good night's sleep.

Elizabeth went to her doctor the next week. Fortunately, her doctor was competent and thorough. He listened to her story of anxiety and fearfulness, but with a high index of suspicion that her problem was more than nerves, he performed a complete physical examination and completed some screening laboratory tests to ascertain the diagnosis.

Elizabeth had hyperthyroidism. The thyroid gland, located in the neck, weighs less than an ounce, but it produces thyroxin and triiodothyronine, two hormones which have an enormous impact on health. When produced in excess they cause, among other symptoms, a rapid heart rate, increased metabolism and rapid burning of calories, weight loss, sweating, nervousness, anxiety, a fine tremor of the hands, fatigue, and difficulty sleeping. Clearly, these are symptoms of severe anxiety disorders, but hyperthyroidism is not a mental health problem. It is a medical problem caused by a broken body part and is amenable to surgery and medication.

A broken body part. Surgery and medication. Science. In any area of specialization, the special language can be a barrier to "outsiders." We referred to that in our introduction. But we must point out that precise vocabulary can also be vital in communication, so we don't want to be reverse-snobs by ruling out such terms. We all know hundreds, if not thousands, of people's names. We don't have to say, "The man with the funny gray spot limited to the hair on his right temple, with a round face and a hairy mole on his left cheek and a little bit of a wall-eye." No, we say "John" and get on with it. Names are very useful. So we ask you to follow along in the next few pages. If it helps, try to forget that what follows is science and just think of it as a fascinating story.

To rephrase the chapter subtitle, the authors might have asked, "How are the lower orders of animals different from human beings?" Well, we're certainly alike in many, many ways. With the caveat that, as authors, we don't warm to words like *all* or *never*, for purposes of illustration let's talk about the ways in which most all animals are alike. All animals have alimentary canals—each comprised of an esophagus, stomach, and bowel. And this canal does the same thing in each animal. It channels nutrients for absorption and waste products for elimination. All animals have hearts and blood vessels that circulate nutrients and oxygen. All animals have skeletal systems, and their bones are alike in how they look and what they do (form and function). All animals have muscles spanning the skeletal system, which makes movement possible. All animals have an adrenal gland that makes epinephrine, a powerful hormone. Brains, lungs, eyes, ears, livers, ovaries, testes—the list in comparative anatomy and comparative function goes on and on.

Furthermore, the fields of biochemistry, physiology, and cellular biology have teased out the elements that make up a living cell (including carbon, nitrogen, hydrogen, and others). Researchers have identified the chemical combinations that make up the amino acids, proteins, and molecules of living cells. They have identified the deoxyribonucleic acids that form the DNA molecules of genes, and they have visualized the double helix structure of genes and modeled the human genome that is the basis of heredity. They have charted the biological pathways that break down sugar, construct hemoglobin, and form urine. We must note that in all animals, these metabolic processes are pretty much the same.

So how are animals and human beings different? In the context of this book, we must certainly reiterate, "Human beings worry!" We know animals communicate and have feelings. They make sounds that mean something to their kith and kin, and if domesticated, they love their masters and mistresses. Do they worry? It's hard to say, but from the way their brains are put together, it's doubtful that they experience the worry and existential angst of humans.

Animals live in communities, just like humans. Bats live in colonies, lions live in prides, and gazelles in herds. The bat has sharper hearing than humans and was flying when we could only gaze wistfully at the sky. The lion, ferocious in tooth and claw, was the supreme hunter in its habitat, but was bested by gunpowder. The gazelle was unmatched in speed and agility—but its graceful bound couldn't take it much beyond the deserts and grasslands of Africa and Asia. Animals are fascinating and remarkable as they swim, scamper, burrow, run, and leap through their environments. But they were trapped by nature in their times and places. No animals developed a civilization! That, we think, is what makes human beings different from lower orders of animals.

Unlike animals, the human being is not just a creature in a landscape. Human beings explore and shape their landscapes, and they have made their home on every continent and in every kind of environment, hospitable and inhospitable. Humankind, through subtlety, imagination, creativity, penetrating thought, organizational skills, and yes, a fierce toughness, changed their environments. True, such change has not always been for the better. Nevertheless, it has been shaped by the hands of humans (the only critters who can nimbly appose their thumb tips to each of their fingertips) and driven by human brains capable of abstract thought.

Animals leave behind bones, but no other traces of who or what they were. Human beings leave behind bones, too, but they also leave behind evidence of civilizations. They leave behind tools of their trades, weapons of war, musical instruments, objects of art, and cathedrals. If you want to know about ancient bats, you study their skeletons and plow through bat guano. If you want to know about ancient humans, you study skeletons, but you also dig up ancient cities.

Civilization is the handiwork of the human brain in all of its remarkable complexity. And civilization, in part, was driven by worry. Where will we find food? Will there be enough food? Where will we find shelter? How can we be safe from animal predators? Human predators? My man did not return from the hunt. What am I going to do? What strategies will we devise to protect us from various threats? If we want to know about humanity and worry, we had better start with the brain science of the human species.

An Overview of the Human Brain

In the beginning was the **amygdala**. It's about the size and shape of an almond, and its name is simply a transliteration of the Greek word for "almond." Very scientific! The amygdala is a tiny chemical factory that sits atop the spinal chord and churns out serotonin, norepinephrine, dopamine, and cortisol. The function of this little lump of tissue is pure reflex—all reaction, no thought. It triggers vegetative responses (like licking, chewing, sucking, and root-ing) and produces primitive emotions (such as fear, panic, rage, and aggression). It produces a thoughtless, hardwired, hair-trigger, lightning-fast chain reaction to any threat, real or perceived. To tweak a colorful phrase from the Old West, "The amygdala shoots first—and never asks any questions."

The amygdala is the total brain of the rattlesnake. But as we ascend the hierarchical ladder of animal life, we find that the amyg-dala acquires additional layers of brain matter that coats it, plumps it up, and fills it out. This adds complexity in anatomy and function. The skull becomes progressively larger and shaped differently to accom-modate more brain tissue. The shovel-shaped skull of the gorilla gives way to the rounded and bulging skull of the human being.

The amygdala, embedded deep in the mid-brain, is surrounded by a cauliflower-like shell called the **cerebrum.** The cerebrum's bulk makes up about four-fifths of the mass of the human brain. It's divided into two halves (or hemispheres, right and left). The outer rim of the cerebrum (also known as the cerebral cortex) is composed of microscopic nerve cell bodies (neurons), and this tissue is gray in color (hence, it is commonly called "gray matter"). Below the cerebral cortex are microscopic thin fibers (axons) that carry messages between neurons throughout the brain and spinal cord. These fibers form dense bands that are white in color (hence, "white matter"). The cerebral cortex has specific areas that manage specialized tasks.

The **frontal lobe** of the cerebral cortex is situated at the front of the brain and sits directly behind the forehead (the bulging, rounded human skull). The frontal lobe controls rational thought, concentration, planning, envisioning the future, problem solving, and multitasking.

The **sensory cortex** of the cerebral hemispheres is located along the back rim of the cerebral cortex and sits inside the rear of the skull. It interprets information from the five senses (sight, smell, hearing, taste, and touch). Working together with other parts of the brain, the sensory cortex interprets and acts on incoming stimuli. A key function is to distinguish genuine threats from false alarms.

The **motor cortex** of the cerebral hemispheres lies along both sides of the brain, resting against the right and left sides of the skull. It sends signals to muscles that control voluntary movement. Interestingly, the control center for the thumb takes up an extraordinarily large area of the motor cortex—larger than the area that controls the entire torso.

The **cerebellum** (Latin for "little brain") is a small ball of tissue about the size of an orange that is nestled under the cerebral hemispheres at the base of the brain. It's located atop the mid-brain (which, remember, contains the amygdala). The cerebellum coordinates learning and controls complicated functions of balance (much like a gyroscope). It gauges the spatial relationship of various parts of the body in relation to the whole body, comparing what you intended to do (a command from the motor cortex) to what you are actually doing. It fine-tunes these movements in split-second adjustments through intricate feedback mechanisms that act as both throttle and brake. Without the cerebellum, we couldn't really *do* anything: use a pencil, drink a cup of coffee, swing a golf club, make pottery, ride a bike, walk a fence rail, catch a ball, or pilot a supersonic airplane.

Having identified the general layers of the brain and broadly defined their functions, we have moved from the surface of the brain to its central core, dissecting through gray and white matter to arrive back at the beginning—the **amygdala**. It still lurks there, a functioning part of the human brain, still doing its primitive thing, reacting without thinking to real and/or perceived threats. It is linked to all parts and areas of the brain both anatomically (through neurons) and chemically (through serotonin, dopamine, norepinephrine, cortisol, and other chemicals).

Cellular biologists (and others) tell us certain single cells (**neurons**) are the functioning units of the human brain. Each neuron has its own brain (**nucleus**) and its own body parts (**dendrites** and **axons**). The dendrites have tiny receptors (think eyes and ears) to receive stimuli from other neurons, and a long axon (think arm and hand) that reaches out to other neurons to pass on a message. An axon may be a fraction of an inch in length or several feet. It may connect with a single neuron or innumerable neurons.

The **neuron**, with its brain and body parts, doesn't actually "think." A neuron is like a switch, either "on" or "off." The neurons sit passively "off," but alive and waiting for a stimulus from another neuron that will turn them "on." And the neurons, with their dendrites and axons, don't actually touch each other. They don't nudge each other in the dark and say, "Psssttt!" to pass on the message. There are tiny gaps (**synapses**) between all neurons. The mediators of each message are chemicals that are collectively called **neurotransmitters**. An electrical discharge within a neuron triggers the release of its neurotransmitters from storage tanks at the end of the axon. They flow into the gap where they are picked up by specific receptors in the dendrite(s) of the recipient neuron(s). That neuron is turned "on," discharging its electrical impulse down its axon to release its neurotransmitters and continue the cascade of messaging. After the recipient dendrite picks up the neurotransmitter to turn the cell "on," it releases the neurotransmitter back into the gap where it is selectively reabsorbed by the prior messaging axon. What causes the initial discharge of an electrical impulse? A stimulus from outside the human body, received via eye, ear, taste, touch, or smell. This ebb and flow of electricity and the release and uptake of chemicals are the "jolt and juice" that keep neurons communicating.

The system is, in many ways, complex beyond comprehension. Not only in how it actually works, but more essentially in what its "cellular life" causes to happen within and among human beings.

We must emphasize that the well-oiled brain (just a body organ) is not controlled by a tiny, brilliant, human geek, sitting in some command module in an ergonomic chair, wearing white socks, Crocs, and sweat pants, a slide-rule dangling from his skinny hips and a T-shirt silk-screened with the words "I think, therefore I am!" No. So what are we to conclude?

Current men and women of science attempt to explain (to the best of their ability), having drawn on the imagination and scientific principles discovered over thousands of years by other men and women of science, what the brain is made of and how it works. And it boggles the mind!

You will recall that we said the functioning widget of the brain is a single cell—the **neuron**. The brain contains about *one hundred billion* neurons. Just think of it! This three-pound mass of tissue, electrically charged and awash in chemicals, is central to seeing, breathing, eating, moving, and sex. But beyond these elementary, almost reflexive functions, the brain allows human beings to create art, pose a theorem, and experience joy, curiosity, apathy, delusions, rage, and anxiety.

Humanity in Sunlight and Darkness

Based on this quick, if technical, overview, we understand that this juiced, jolted, gray and white matter is the *basis of civilization*. Streaming from this marvelous organ is the wheel and the space station. The axe and the nuclear weapon. The privy and the cathedral. Chess and tiddlywinks. The drum and the violin. The garage band and the marching band. "You Ain't Nothin' But A Hound Dog" and the *Jupiter* Symphony. Heidelberg Castle and the Holocaust. Mother Teresa (with all her good works and all of her doubts) and Jeffrey Dahmer (and whatever went on, tragically, with his neurons and neurotransmitters). As well as the calm and serene individual and the worrywart.

Throughout the progress of civilization, the higher centers of the **cerebral cortex** are interacting with the primitive, still-functioning **amygdala**, trying to keep a lid on things. The control mechanisms always function secondarily, after the amygdala's "shoot first," panicked response. The control mechanisms may plug in inadequately, a split second late or not at all. We *know* all of this, but we don't *really know*! It's a miracle.

Human beings who are fortunate have brains that are in reasonably good working order. Experience has shown we should discount the idea of perfect working order. Brains that are most of the time in good working order allow us to function in this complex world. For those human beings whose brains are in poor working order, including those with crippling anxiety and destructive worry, modern science believes that the primitive mid-brain remains as a vestige of our primal selves. Worry and anxiety are the direct descendents of fear and panic, reflexes spilling over into our twenty-first-century lives.

Humankind in the Shadows

Natural science believes the anatomical and physiological fountainhead of worry and anxiety is the brain, specifically the primitive mid-brain. When the finely tuned, coordinated, responsive process of the smoothly functioning brain that can create the *Jupiter* Symphony goes awry, it produces off-key Chopsticks. Perhaps even off-key Chopsticks played over and over and over again. In the terms of health and wellness, this malfunction is a malady (an illness) that causes us to be uneasy (dis-ease).

Diseases have symptoms and manifestations that may be physical, psychological, social, and spiritual. It is to these concerns that we now turn.

Chapter Four

WORRIED SICK

The Pathology of Worry and Anxiety

"I must slip off to the woods to worry. I must
go away with my terrors until I have
taught them to sing."

—W. H. Auden, "The Age of Anxiety"

Jane had always been a tidy person, committed to order, timeliness, and good personal hygiene. Under increasing stress at work and fearful of downsizing in her company and the possibility of losing her job, her feelings of impending disaster began to intensify. These feelings expanded beyond work-related issues and began to intrude into her thoughts on other matters. She became worried about germs making her sick and contaminating her environment. She couldn't seem to stop obsessing about becoming ill and life simply flying out of control. The more she tried to control the constant fear generated by excessive negative thinking, always expecting the worst to happen, the more frightened she became.

Jane took action. And then more action. And then unrelenting repeated action. She developed the habit of constant and compulsive hand washing. Everything in her house was repeatedly cleaned and organized. Nothing was allowed to be out of place. Her life could be described as "much ado about nothing" or "much ado about everything" in her attempt to stave off disaster by "magical means." Life became more and more difficult, isolating, and threatening. Her social life became increasingly constricted and controlled by her obsessions. Her behaviors became not free choices or reasoned actions but compulsions.

Jane was suffering from obsessive-compulsive disorder. She had developed obsessions that were followed by compulsions, performed almost in a ritualistic manner in order to prevent disaster. Obsessive-compulsive behavior is one of the ways we can become "worried sick."

᠁ ᠁ ᠁

We tend to think of worry and anxiety as something "in the mind." And it is, because as we have discussed, worry (fear's twin) is hard-wired in the brain. But importantly, worry is also "in the body."

Physical Manifestations of Worry

The cascade of neural arcs, chemicals, and electrical impulses that churn in the brain when we are frightened or worried also churn throughout the body. Again, as noted earlier, when we perceive danger (for instance, when an oncoming car swerves over into our traffic lane), our bodies react instantaneously and without our conscious control. Our pupils dilate, our heart rates increase, our blood pressure goes up; we breathe faster; hearing, smell, and skin sensation is more acute, digestion grinds to a halt, and sugar stores are released to energize the muscles. Every molecule of our physical and mental resources is fired up to counter the threat. When the risk subsides and our bodies go off red alert, everything winds down. We are usually exhausted, physically and mentally.

Well, the brain does the same thing to our body when we worry. The initial reaction isn't a lightning flash, but a long, slow burn (of which we may not even be aware), and yet, the involuntary physical output of worry mirrors the processes our bodies undergo in response to fear. It is little wonder that worry causes us to be both physically and mentally drained.

Psychological Manifestations of Worry

Worry is expressed in various ways and to varying degrees. Excessive worry may simply be a nuisance that limits our ability to live and work and play efficiently. It detracts from a smooth, energetic quality of life. Thus worry spills over into our **social** selves with detrimental effects. Worry may weigh us down with guilt and spill over into our **spiritual** selves with a burdened religion. Irrational and obsessive worry may become so distorted and pathological that it becomes a part of a diagnosable mental illness.

Mental Illness and Destructive Worry

In the field of mental illness, panic attacks are the biological and psychological building blocks of syndromes that extend beyond ordinary worry to distinct malfunctions of the mind. A panic attack is defined as a discrete period of intense fear or discomfort, building in a rapid crescendo, which contains at least four of the following symptoms.

- Pounding heart and rapid heart rate
- Sweating
- Trembling and shaking
- Shortness of breath or smothering feelings
- Choking sensations
- Chest pain

- Nausea or abdominal distress
- Dizziness, lightheadedness, or feeling faint
- Feelings of unreality or being detached from one's self
- Fear of losing control or "going crazy"
- Fear of imminent death
- Numbness and tingling sensations in the body
- Chills or hot flashes

By itself, a panic attack (an episode containing four or more of these symptoms) is not a specific category of mental illness that stands alone as a distinct diagnosis. We have all experienced a panic attack under certain stressful situations: an oncoming automobile swerves into our lane of traffic, or a figure suddenly appears from a dark alley when we are walking alone at night. Such events engage our fight-or-flight responses and are easily explained by the immediate cause. True panic attacks occur without a known stimulus, tend to recur in inexplicable fashion, and are always part of other illnesses listed in the *Diagnostic and Statistical Manual of Mental Illness*, fourth edition, or DSM-IV, the Bible of mental illness for health professionals. The DSM-IV contains two general headings under which panic attacks are diagnosed: anxiety disorders and mood disorders.

One such diagnosis is panic disorder. This illness is characterized by recurrent, unexplained panic attacks that are not due to substance abuse (i.e. caffeine, amphetamines, recreational drugs, alcohol, hallucinogens, inhalants, or prescription drugs).

Another such diagnosis is general anxiety disorder. GAD is characterized by at least six months of intermittent panic attacks and persistent and excessive anxiety and worry. This illness contains the following features:

- Excessive worry occurring more often than not for a six-month period
- Difficulty in controlling or abating worry

- Anxiety and worry associated with at least three of
  the following symptoms more often than not over six
  months:
    * Restlessness, or feeling "keyed up"
    * Fatigue
    * Difficulty concentrating
    * Irritability
    * Muscle tension
    * Sleep disturbances (difficulty falling asleep or
      staying asleep, or experiencing restless, unsatisfy-
      ing sleep)

Furthermore, in GAD:

- Anxiety and worry cause clinically significant distress
  and impair social or occupational functioning.
- The focus of anxiety is not defined by or linked to
  other forms of anxiety (that is, the person in question is not anxious about having recurrent panic
  attacks, which would point not to GAD, but to panic
  disorder), being embarrassed in public (as in social
  disorder), being contaminated by germs or radiation
  (as in obsessive-compulsive disorder), or associated
  with various physical complaints (as in somatization
  disorder).
- Anxiety and worry are not present as a result of substance abuse, general medical conditions, or a mood
  or psychotic disorder.

Another specific diagnosis that includes the symptoms of panic
attacks and destructive worry is Anxiety Disorder Due To General
Medical Conditions. Chronic, free-floating anxiety should prompt
you to visit your personal physician to discuss your symptoms and

have a thorough physical examination. In these cases, the physician will include the diagnosis of anxiety disorder under the primary illness. Medical conditions in which anxiety is a direct consequence of the physical illness are:

- Hyperthyroidism—excessive production of thyroid hormone
- Hyperparathyroidism—excessive production of parathyroid hormone
- Pheochromocytoma—a tumor of the adrenal glands producing increased quantities of adrenalin and cortisone
- Hypoadrenocorticism—low levels of adrenalin and cortisone
- Seizure disorders
- Heart disease—arrhythmias, supraventricular tachycardia
- Hypoglycemia—low blood sugar
- Pulmonary embolism—blood clots from veins that lodge in the lungs
- Chronic Obstructive Pulmonary Disease—difficulty breathing leading to lack of oxygen
- Metabolic conditions—vitamin B12 deficiency, abnormal products of red blood cell breakdown circulating in the blood stream
- Neurological conditions—brain tumors, vestibular dysfunction, encephalitis

Finally, there are other categories of mental illness under which panic attacks and destructive worry are included, and these include:

- Panic attacks with phobias
  (A phobia being the fear and avoidance of a specific thing or circumstance.)
- Post-traumatic stress disorder

- Obsessive-compulsive disorder
- Attention deficit disorder
- Separation anxiety disorder
  (Usually occurs in children.)
- Paranoia
- Schizophrenia
- Major depression
  (Also known as unipolar disorder.)
- Manic depression
  (Also known as bipolar disorder.)

This material from DSM-IV gives us insight into the broad range of anxiety disorders associated with a "broken brain." This is clearly a complicated subject and these diagnoses are listed here only for a comprehensive overview. It is left for psychiatrists, psychologists, and other mental health professionals, in conjunction with general physicians, to classify each illness as it relates to a person's specific symptoms.

For the moment, though, we should return to the majority of people who don't fit into the specific, codified diagnoses of mental illnesses set forth in the DSM-IV. These people are plagued by shades of worry from the occasional, specific, distressing worry to persistent, heightened, long-lasting, unremitting anxiety. Just as a muscle can "spasm" (cramp up painfully and not let go), the mind also can "spasm." Time—hours, days, weeks, months, even years—can be ruined by a worry that one can't release. And if the worrying mind remains cramped, the mind can become scratched, like an old vinyl record. The record player's needle is repetitively shunted back to its old hurtful groove and can't trace the disk's normal pattern. The worried mind responds to this recording glitch by continually stimulating the body with neurotransmitters and hormones. Such persons are always in the fight-or-flight mode. These reactions in both the mind and the body, unless altered with therapy, can become permanent and harmful.

Yet, there is hope when one begins to distinguish between destructive worry and smart worry, between the neurotic fear that paralyzes and the wise fear that motivates. This is why it is important to educate one's self in the nature of worry in all its dimensions—biological, spiritual and psychological—and helpful to engage with others in supportive conversation or to seek pastoral or therapeutic help in recognizing one's location on the worry scale. To live "hope-in-action" is a key dynamic in the process that is both healing and redemptive. Thus we turn in the next chapter to handling ordinary worry.

Chapter Five

HANDLING ORDINARY WORRY

Training Yourself for Healing

"I've looked over, and I've seen the promised
land . . . . So I'm happy tonight. I'm not
worried about anything. I'm not fearing any man."

—Martin Luther King, Jr., address to striking sanitation workers, Memphis

Paul was going out less and less. He avoided as many social situations as he could, especially parties. He hated "playing party games," engaging in small talk, and "mingling." It wasn't just that he didn't enjoy himself. He was actually afraid to go out. It filled him with dread and anxiety. He feared looking like a fool or being humiliated in the public setting. He felt exposed to criticism and negative evaluation. He would seek any reason or make any excuse to stay at home. What made it even worse is that he knew there was really no rational reason for his fear.

Paul's wife cajoled him, supported him, reasoned with him, encouraged him, and prodded him, but to no avail. Her patience was running out. A toll was being taken on their friendships, and for no reason as far as she could see. Paul knew it, was embarrassed by it, and wanted to change. But his fear was too great.

Paul was suffering from social phobia. He was not just "shy." He had an irrational fear of harmless situations that filled him with such anxiety that his life and his marriage were adversely affected. His overbearing self-consciousness kept him from functioning freely. There are a number of specific phobias recognized as anxiety disorders. Among the more common phobias are fear of enclosed places, fear of open spaces, fear of animals, fear of heights, fear of flying, fear of bridges or tunnels, and fear of water.

We must remind ourselves again that our goal is not to eliminate worry. Such a goal is not only impossible because of our biology, but would be detrimental because of our needs. Worry alerts us to problems or danger and demands that we attend to them. It is only when wise worry morphs into destructive worry that it holds the past, present and future hostage. The past stalks us with the fear that something will sneak up from behind and strike us down. The future haunts us with the fear of unknown disasters. Past and future squeeze the life out of the present with anxiety.

As we've said before, people are worriers. If we try to gauge our own location on the worry scale—from situational worrier, to worrywart, to destructive worrier—it's really not too hard to know where we fit. We basically know if we move along comfortably from day to day and slip into worry when confronted by a situation that demands it. We also have pretty good insight into whether we are always gnawing at some problem—and if, when it passes, we fasten onto another concern. And we generally know if they are destructive worries, clinging to inventions of our imagination.

Destructive worry is usually not about the realities of our world, but it bubbles up from within us. It saps our energy, subverts productive thought, and steals away the time. Family, friends, work, and play all become enmeshed in the process. The person with destructive worry suffers mentally and physically. Mental suffering may become a mental illness. Physical suffering can become a physical illness. And the pathology of worry in a person inevitably spills over into disturbed social relationships—between wives and husbands, parents and children, colleagues at work, and friends.

Wherever we fit on the worry scale, we must acknowledge our worrisome self and manage it. If we see we are slipping toward destructive worry, we must short-circuit it before mental or physical illness occurs. So the important question is, how do we do these things?

Handling Ordinary Worry before It Becomes Destructive Worry

The first rule of managing worry is learning to *distinguish* between smart worry and destructive worry. It doesn't take a genius to do this, and it should only take a moment. Having said that, some people apparently don't have the insight to make that distinction. Telling someone afflicted with destructive worry "not to worry" does as much good as telling a rock it is a bird. Such persons have deeper underlying psychological, social, spiritual problems that require a different approach. But for those "marginal worrywarts," there is a moment, a critical time period, when they are able to abort the spiral of emotions and physical symptoms heading down into destructive worry.

Worry is a symptom. Physicians regard a symptom as a warning sign of an illness and are taught to evaluate symptoms in a systematic manner. In recent years, the method of evaluation has been fixed by following an acronym: SOAP. This is a little too cute for old-fashioned doctors, especially with the implication that it will clean things right up, but SOAP has a simple logic to it for solving a problem. The letters stand for:

Subjective

Objective

Assessment

Plan

In the **Subjective** stage of evaluating a condition, the doctor must first listen to the patient's complaint or story and get it straight. Patients commonly criticize doctors for not listening. It's a valid criticism, and medicine is the poorer for it. But that's not the way it should be or was meant to be. The physician author of this book remembers his mentor in physical diagnosis, Dr. Mahlon Delp, medical clinician and diagnostician *par excellence*, saying that doctors must *listen* to patients and they would *tell* their own diagnoses. Many practicing physicians today take that listening approach, and there is renewed emphasis in medicine on the patient's story (symptoms of the illness, length of time symptoms have been present, how they began, what makes them better and worse, and all of the other narrative features that define an illness) in making an accurate diagnosis. Such listening also creates a bond that establishes trust and prepares the ground for providing therapy.

Once the patient has shared his or her perspective and experiences, the physician must do a careful physical examination and note the **Objective** findings. These findings, both positive and negative, must be thoroughly assessed and integrated into the patient's story. Only then does the doctor have sufficient information to **Assess** the problem and make a diagnosis, which leads directly to a **Plan** to care for the patient and alleviate the illness and its symptoms.

Even outside of the doctor's office, when you are confronted by a specific worry, the fundamental thing you must do is confront your worry and **SOAP** it!

Subjective

Identify your worry and name it. If you can't name the causes of your anxiety, your worry is free-floating. This is a more serious mental health issue and requires professional treatment. We will discuss professional therapy for destructive worry in the next chapter, but our focus now is helping the basic worrier.

First, there are worries that are sudden and compelling. They precipitate a feeling of crisis. Examples of such worries are:

- Your ten-year-old daughter is an hour late getting home from grade school and you have heard nothing.
- You are driving alone on a highway at night and your oil gauge light comes on.
- You receive a notice from your bank informing you that your account has insufficient funds and they are stopping payment on your checks.
- Your employer tells you the company is downsizing by thirty percent over the next three months, and they are considering eliminating your position.

Then, there are worries that are chronic and nagging. Examples are:

- You have pain in your belly that has been coming and going for several months.
- You have been trying to reach a good friend for several weeks. Your friend doesn't answer your e-mails or letters, and calls you leave on the answering machine go unreturned.
- Your doctoral committee has rejected three revisions of your dissertation, and you feel six years of work slipping away from you.
- You suspect your spouse is having an affair.

Once you have named your worry, you have subjectively identified your symptom and told its story.

Objective

Second, be objective! Get the facts relevant to your worry. Without facts, the imagination magnifies any problem. Get busy (one of the single most empowering things you can do) and track down all the necessary information. Depending on the problem that needs researching, the computer-literate person can easily Google for quick information. Otherwise, use books and the services of appropriate organizations. Track down experts in the field. Consult friends who are reliable and knowledgeable.

Break the worry down into its various parts. Weigh and measure each part. Place a value on each part of the problem to understand its significance. Establish a priority for working on each part of the problem to find a solution. The priority might be based on the more weighty matters, but not necessarily. It may be important to address lesser issues first, either to give clarity to what is considered a more significant issue or perhaps to clear away the underbrush and simplify the task of addressing the worry.

For example, having a ten-year-old daughter who is significantly late getting home from school is worrisome. The worry might be analyzed and prioritized as follows:

1. Is the neighborhood considered safe or are there known to be problem areas or people?
2. Does the daughter have a health problem (diabetes or a seizure disorder) that may affect her ability to function?
3. Has the daughter ever been late before? If so, why?
4. Does the daughter have a habit of being late?
5. If the daughter is late, does she usually call home?

6. Did the parent forget that the daughter had an activity after school?

7. Is the daughter's teacher always punctual with class time?

8. Is the daughter's teacher always careful for the safety of each child?

9. Is the principal attentive to students as they leave school each day?

10. How does the daughter get to and from school each day? Does she walk, car pool, ride a school bus, or use public transportation?

Assess

Take steps to solve the problem without delay. If you don't, your imagination will ricochet from one disaster to another. Use the information you have gathered from your objective fact-finding. Information that is placed on the shelf quickly gathers dust and is useless. It does you no good unless you use it to set in motion a plan of action to address the problem. And remember, it's wise not to worry alone. The old adage "Two heads are better than one" is true in most cases. Immediately request help and get support from a relative, trusted neighbor, or friend.

With regard to the tardy daughter:

1. There are no known problems or people in the neighborhood. Million to one chance anything sinister has befallen the daughter. Postpone calling the police, and don't panic!

2. The daughter does not have a health problem. A sudden acute illness or accident would be rare. Worry about calling hospital emergency rooms or urgent care centers much later.

3. The daughter is rarely more than a few minutes late from school. She knows it would worry her parents.
4. Being home late from school is not a chronic problem.
5. The daughter is good about getting to a telephone in emergencies or unusual circumstances and informing her mother.

Issues 1 through 5 takes ten seconds. Disaster scenarios may still nag the parent, but he or she must quickly move on.

6. The parent does not know of any after-school activity for the day.
7-9. The daughter's teacher and principal are both conscientious about time and safety.
10. The parent knows the daughter walks to and from school with friends.

Five more seconds have passed.

Plan

The parent, together with a friend or neighbor, sets about the tasks necessary to resolve the outstanding questions from her assessment.

1. The parent double-checks the calendar that is scribbled full of appointment dates, activities, and chores. There is nothing listed for today.
2. The parent immediately calls the house of one of the daughter's friends. That child came home from school on time and says that the daughter did not walk home with their usual group. The parent's anxiety level goes up.
3. The parent calls the school administrator's office and asks to speak with principal, who believes the

daughter is in the gym with other students practicing the program for the school's fiftieth anniversary
celebration. There was a memo with that information
last week. Parent's worry turns to embarrassment
remembering the neglected memo. Principal agrees to
go down to the gym and check on the situation, then
calls back to confirm the daughter's presence. Parent
heaves a big sigh of relief and makes a cup of tea.

When you worry, as silly as it may sound, try SOAP. Subjectively
identify your worry! Objectively analyze it! Assess what needs to be
done to fix it! Act on your Plan immediately! Don't hold on to your
worry as if it is the end and not the means to resolution! Planning,
organization, and simple action carries us a long way to disposing
of ordinary worries. We are then free to turn our attention to other
daily tasks. Many people do this almost automatically, but if you
don't, you can train yourself.

If the practical steps outlined here aren't enough, you may
be dealing with a more severe pattern of destructive worry. The
situation may not be a diagnosable mental health disorder, but it
still requires a different approach than the practical steps outlined
above, and these approaches can be taken in therapy.

Chapter Six

MANAGING DESTRUCTIVE WORRY

General Principles

"You alone can do it, but you cannot do it alone."

—O. Hobart Mower

J ared was excited about his new job. He felt energized and confident on the first day as he drove to work. He knew he could perform with exceptional proficiency as a medical records clerk for this group of hospital-based radiologists. He had a business degree from Missouri State University. He was punctual, reliable, meticulous, and well-organized. "Just the kind of attributes this job requires," the office manager had said when she hired him. His only anxiety was that she had looked at him with just the slightest hint of misgiving when she had offered him the position at the close of his second call-back interview. He knew he would have to be especially circumspect with her and give her no cause to express her reservations about him. Moreover, there was a long-term employee in medical records that he would have to keep his eye on. She had seniority in the department, but he knew he was a threat to her because of his excellent qualifications. After the office manager had introduced him to the other employees at the close of his last interview, he later saw this woman speaking quietly to another man. She definitely had his ear, and they had both smiled knowingly as they glanced in his direction. He would need to remain aloof and keep his own counsel so they couldn't undermine his performance. He knew how to manage this, he told himself. He had dealt with it before.

Jared's enthusiasm gave way to anxiety as he turned into the hospital parking lot. This job with the radiologists was his seventh job since he had graduated from college five years previously. He had not only changed jobs because of the injustices he had suffered, but he had moved twice to different communities in order to distance himself from employers who, because of their antagonism, might write critical letters of recommendation. This time, he thought uneasily, he must overcome every obstacle that anyone placed in his way to bar him from success.

Paranoia, with feelings of persecution and an exaggerated sense of self-importance, occurs in many mental disorders, but is often a part of anxiety disorders. The paranoia may be relatively limited and mild, but the feelings often become unshakeable and part of a delusional system. In Jared's case, the feelings are fixed in his mind and severe enough to interfere with his daily life and work.

There are certain realities to the human situation. Added to the biological fact that fear and worry are hardwired into our bodies, life is unfair. Life is capricious. Life is uncertain. There is injustice and betrayal. We are affected by chance, whim, coincidence, providence, and fortune. Some people are able to believe in Divine Providence, live by it, and benefit from the concept. Others find this more difficult; their experiences of life have rendered them incapable of trust or hope. They are constantly fearful and on guard. They no longer trust their common sense or their instincts. It is impossible to say why some people suffer life's outrageous inequities and are able to get on with their lives while others are permanently impaired. But one of the realities of the human situation is that some people are simply unable to do life's heavy lifting. Having said that, most people have more personal resources than they give themselves credit for.

As we have discussed, we are dealing with the mind and psychology and with the body and physiology. Mind and body are both intimately involved with worry, and there is no separating them. Some skeptics dismiss psychology as mind games and psychobabble. They write off physiology as a way of blaming pre-determined fate and seizing a "get out of jail free" pass to avoid responsibility. They urge toughness and discipline. The words of the poet W. E. Henley might be their mantra: "I am the master of my fate; I am the captain of my soul." And such skeptics make a point. People, including worriers, do need toughness and discipline.

While we're speaking of skepticism and solutions to problems, we should say that yes, people should be skeptical of "quick fixes." If something seems too easy or too good to be true, it most probably is. Be wary of the "trendy" (apricot pits to cure cancer), "bumper sticker" philosophies ("When the going gets tough, the tough get going"), your best friend's admonitions ("You're your own worst enemy"), bootstrap advice ("Just get a grip"), and magical religion ("You've got to pray hard").

There is no one, single therapy that is always effective in treating destructive worry. Usually, as with most illnesses, a combination of therapies is most effective. We the authors believe that human beings are body, mind, and spirit, and that we live and grow in our unique racial, geographic, political, historical, economic, social, and religious settings. Together, these all influence behavior. It should not be surprising that the treatment of destructive worry encompasses medicine, psychology, and religion, and that specific individual and social circumstances must be taken into account.

General Principles for Managing Destructive Worry

Before we turn to specific therapies for destructive worry, let's talk about some general principles that help overcome it. First and foremost, we must remember that there are better solutions to destructive worry than simply "bearing up." Medical problems require diagnosis and medical treatment. Psychological problems require mental health therapy. Spiritual problems require religious insight and spiritual direction. Above all, we must realize that we must be nursed back to health. This phrase has fallen out of use in this day of instant gratification. Recovering our health takes time. Further, the term "health" is a relative one. Very few people, if any, are in perfect health. They learn to live with their infirmities. They manage to accommodate them. Those with chronic illnesses—diabetes, heart disease, ulcerative colitis, asthma—follow an extended regimen of treatment and learn to avoid those factors that aggravate their diseases.

Another general principle of managing worry is to learn skills that help. People learn skills throughout their lives, from perfecting an accurate tennis serve, to flying an airplane, to playing a piano, to knitting, to managing mental health problems. There are, of course, people with natural talent. They possess a native ability to excel at certain things. They have a leg-up on the average person trying to perform the same skill or accomplish the same task. But we have a friend who was a basketball player who confided to us, "You know my natural jump shot? I practiced that shot tens of thousands of times, starting as a kid in my back yard with a hoop that didn't have a net." A baseball player with a natural talent for pitching still learns how to put a certain spin on a ball to add to his repertoire of pitches. It takes work and lots of practice. A good surgeon has some natural aptitude for the vocation. To begin with, it helps not to throw up at the sight of blood or get the shakes when picking up a scalpel, though these things also can be learned and desensitization does occur. On the other hand, surgeons learn anatomy to find their way around a body. They learn techniques (placing sutures or using an endoscopic tool) that are perfected by repetition. Practice helps make perfect, and it does so by using repetitive motions to develop "muscle" memory. The best surgeons have superior judgment, but that too is learned by acquiring experience. People who suffer from destructive worry can learn to put a certain spin on their brain, acquire new management techniques, store up knowledge, accumulate experience, and develop brain-muscle memory. A professional in any field is someone who can do superior work with inadequate tools under adverse conditions when they don't feel like it, and take responsibility for the results. People can become a professional at working through destructive worry by building skills that lead to reliable expertise.

In general, the most effective machinery for handling and defusing destructive worry (or almost any mental health problem) is a good support system. We must be deeply and actively connected to people, places, institutions, and ideas. Spouses, children, and extended family are vital connections to life and health. Good friends stand next in line. Neighbors, colleagues, comrades, teammates, coaches, teachers, doctors, counselors, and spiritual leaders are invaluable in a support system. Make careful choices about who you talk to. They should be age-appropriate and capable of keeping confidences, and they should have sound judgment. Communication with a life companion, relatives, and friends is not necessarily about finding a solution to a problem, but about experiencing a genuine emotional connection. There is probably nothing more important to human health than human contact. Loneliness is debilitating. Experiments have demonstrated that without contact with their kind, creatures fail to thrive and even waste away and die. Studies have shown that the elderly who live by themselves often visit doctors just to have conversation and experience care and physical touch.

There are also safe places that are indispensable to your life. Admittedly, not every place on the following list is a safe haven for everyone, sadly not even the home. Still, the home, workplace, school, minister's office, priest's confessional, senior centers, union halls, shelters, police precinct, and fire stations can be safe places. Institutions, including clubs, societies, veteran's organizations, business and professional associations, places of worship, twelve-step programs, and specialized support groups are ready resources. The services a 911 telephone call can provide are only moments away. Finally and importantly, a belief system or philosophy (religious, secular, or both) that serves to bring order to our human existence provides stability and hope in a world that is insecure and fragmented.

Taken together, the general principles and connectedness discussed above do three things. First, they place many personal, professional, and institutional resources at our fingertips. Second, they distribute the weight of our troubles. Third, they replace a frightening sense of vulnerability with genuine empowerment.

Chapter Seven

Managing Destructive Worry

Western Therapy

> "Anxiety does not empty tomorrow of its sorrows,
> but only empties today of its strengths."
>
> —Charles Spurgeon

Ruth shut off the alarm clock and remained in bed. She wanted to pull the covers up over her head, but resisted the impulse. Instead, she lay with her hands at her side and planned her day, step by step. Breakfast: wheat toast, yogurt, and coffee. Get ready for work; make the commute. It was her turn to pick up the two other employees in their carpool. She had scheduled lunch with one of the employees, whom she supervised. The woman, a nice enough sort, was half her age but had twice again her credentials. It was tricky, but doable. Afternoon conference with Development and Sales. She was well-prepared for her presentation, but she wasn't a computer whiz. That evening she would prepare her favorite meal ... and dine alone ... again. After that, her book club. All of the activities in the world didn't make up for companionship.

Her husband had died suddenly four years previously. An aortic aneurism. The doctor said he didn't feel a thing. That was the same thing they told her about her son, the victim of an improvised explosive device in Iraq. Her priest listened, consoled and prayed for her. Her psychologist said, "You have really been hammered." Talk and talk every week. Strategies for living. Medication, too, coordinated with her family physician. She remembered what her son had said he told his squad: "Heroism consists of hanging on one minute longer." Ruth swung her feet out of bed and placed them squarely on the floor, feeling her way into her house-slippers. She stood and placed one foot in front of the other and began her day.

Ruth worried, suffered grief, loneliness, and depression, and kept on keeping on.

❧   ❧   ❧

We must now move on to the specifics of treatment for destructive worry. Just as we used the acronym SOAP to help develop strategies to deal with "ordinary" worry, we can use the same acronym to devise a strategy to treat destructive worry. (We will apply this device over both this chapter and the next.) We must remind ourselves that SOAP doesn't eliminate a temperament that worries excessively; instead, it outlines tactics to cope with problems. With intervention and professional help, a destructive worrier can find a passage to a safe harbor.

Subjective

Our own experience tells us that destructive worry harms us. Philosophers would say that is an existential insight. You probably have a reasonable insight into whether or not you are a destructive worrier. But since some people caught in the web of destructive worry lose the ability to make that judgment, here are some questions you can ask yourself that might help clarify your relationship with anxiety:

1. Was worry a constant part of your childhood (worry about your parents and family, school, friendships, possible disasters, or death)?
2. Have you worried all of your life?
3. Are you unable to put worrisome thoughts out of your mind?
4. Do worrisome thoughts distract you from taking care of day–to–day business?
5. Do you fail to complete your daily tasks because you have spent the time worrying about something?
6. If you have finally put to rest a worry that has consumed you, do you immediately take up the thread of another worry?
7. Does the same worry keep intruding itself into your thoughts so that you keep mulling it over and are unable to put it out of your mind?
8. Do friends, close associates or your spouse tell you that you worry too much?
9. Do these same people, when you share your worries, say that your worries are silly or irrational?
10. Is it impossible for you to take joy from simple pleasures because your thoughts are distracted by worry?
11. Does a worry burrow in your mind until you have dug a hole so deep you think you will never heal?
12. Does worry cause you to develop physical symptoms (stomach ache, headache, sweating, pounding heart, rapid pulse, excessive fatigue, loss of appetite, inability to sleep)?

13. When you have a worry, do you constantly fret about it, or do you analyze it and attempt to do something about it to lay it to rest?

14. Do you despair of ever being able to set things right and get on with your life?

15. Are you sad, blue, or depressed most of the time?

16. Do you feel overtaken by obsessive thoughts that you just can't release?

17. Do you turn to alcohol or recreational drugs to take your mind off of your worries?

18. Has your work suffered because of worry?

19. Have you lost jobs, friends, or a spouse because of excessive worry?

20. Does a feeling of panic come over you that seems terrifying and life threatening?

Simply tallying up a "yes" or "no" for each question does not provide a mathematical score that defines your level of worry. Everyone has bad days and some days are worse than others. Certainly, everyone has some of these feelings occasionally. Yet very few emotionally healthy people have many of these feelings regularly, while people who are destructive worriers have a lot of these feelings a lot of the time. Be honest with yourself. You really do have a pretty good insight into how much the "worry pattern" intrudes into your life, how much dis-ease worrying causes you. If you are a person who is overwhelmed or incapacitated by destructive worry, you must get help. That implies treatment. Where should you turn to get objective facts about your health and appropriate therapy?

Objective

When we talk of treatment, we tend to think in terms of doctors and medicine. In Western culture, the term *medicine* has been associated almost exclusively with therapies rooted in the natural sciences and the scientific method—physical examination, laboratory tests, medication, treatments, psychotherapy. There are, however, cultures throughout the world that approach disease and healing with different concepts and methodology. For purposes of this book, we have used the term Complementary and Alternative Therapy (CAT) for these combinations of therapy. CATs range from Eastern traditions thousands of years old (such as acupuncture) to New Age remedies (like crystals). In this chapter, we will discuss Western methods of dealing with destructive worry; we will turn to therapies offered from CAT medicine in the next chapter.

Western Medicine and Therapy for Destructive Worry

The first thing a destructive worrier should do is see a physician for a thorough medical examination. Remember, worry and anxiety are symptoms of many medical conditions; identifying and treating the underlying illness alleviates the symptoms. You must tell your physician about your worry, why you believe it is destructive, and your concerns for your health and mental health. After your consultation and examination, if underlying health problems are diagnosed, you must work with your physician to address them. On the other hand, you may learn that you don't have a physical illness and that you don't fit into a diagnostic category of mental illness. You discover you are simply one of the untold numbers of people who worry too much and inappropriately. With that knowledge and reassurance, what should you do next?

Your own physician may feel in a position to help you, or your physician can refer you to other appropriate professionals. Choices include psychiatrists, psychologists, counselors, ministers, and self-help groups. Singly, or sometimes working together, these therapists and resources can guide you into more constructive thought patterns.

The Use of Medications

Harking back to our discussion of the brain, we remind ourselves that chemicals like serotonin and others, or neurotransmitters, lubricate the transmission of messages along the communication networks between nerve cells. When these chemicals are not present in sufficient amounts, the brain doesn't function well. If destructive worry is associated with diagnosable mental health problems such as depression or obsessive compulsive disorder, medication may be helpful in treating destructive worry. Prozac was the first such drug and remains the classic example embedded in pop culture as the icon of psychiatric drugs. There are many other medicines psychiatrists may use now in addition to Prozac. The exact ways in which these medications work is not important to this discussion. But the fact that they *do* work *is* important, and the fact that there are many different medications allows the therapist to find the one that is most effective for each patient.

Some people may have reservations about taking medications. These reservations extend to all medications of any type, but they are especially pronounced for medicines that affect the brain. Some reservations are psychological: "Taking medicines means I'm weak" or "If I take drugs, I'm admitting I'm sick." Some reservations are spiritual: "Taking a pill means I don't have enough faith." Some are psychosocial: "I don't like to put foreign substances in my body." And still other reservations are physical: "I'm afraid I'll get addicted." Good doctors weigh benefits and risks when prescribing any drug, and inform their patients about side effects. Good doctors monitor their patients for the appearance of side effects. When a doctor says a particular medication will help you and educates you about the risks, discuss it and make an informed decision, but don't refuse to take it just because there might be side effects. After all, every medication has benefits (therapy) and risks (side effects). The package insert on aspirin (a drug so mild it is sold without prescription and several tons of it are taken in America every year) lists ulcers and dangerous bleeding as side effects.

Remember, if your worry is destructive, it is not weak or cheating on life to take appropriate medications. The medication treats an illness, and taking it is no more weak or cheating than taking insulin for diabetes.

Physical Modes of Therapy

If destructive worry *is* associated with depression and medications don't help, physical modes of therapy can be used. This includes electroconvulsive therapy (previously called electroshock therapy) and repeated transcranial magnetic stimulation (RTMS). The application of electric impulses or magnetic stimulation to the brain has a beneficial effect on various mental illnesses, including destructive worry.

Psychotherapy for Destructive Worry

It has long been known that talking out your troubles can be good for you. For ordinary worry this is encapsulated in the phrase, "Don't worry alone." Telling your story to a sympathetic listener assures you that you don't have to worry alone. Advice and talk therapy share common characteristics. Advice, good or bad, tells you what you should do. Therapy goes beyond advice in several ways. Therapy gets the patient involved. Therapy uses tested techniques for self-discovery and problem-solving. Since the nineteenth century, this type of treatment has been termed psychotherapy. Psychotherapy works on the cerebral cortex where learning, concentration, rational thought, planning, and problem-solving reside.

General physicians usually don't have specialized training in psychotherapy, nor do they have adequate time because of busy schedules. Even psychiatrists may not focus on or commit the time necessary for psychotherapy. A psychologist, by training and professional purpose, is ideally suited to provide education, support, insight, objectivity, feedback, understanding, and guidance. A person suffering from destructive worry can, in the presence of a good psychologist, begin the process of understanding what is happening, come to terms with feelings and fears, make emotional adjustments, develop coping strategies, address certain habits and behaviors, deal with relational issues, and find the means for exploring the future with hope.

In addition to the varied skills the psychologist brings to therapy, talking reduces stress and moves the patient along the road to problem-solving. A psychologist can:

- Help prepare a person emotionally for the trial-and-error that is often necessary to finding the most effective medication for that person.
- Encourage compliance in taking medication and provide support in dealing with possible side effects.
- Help the patient make behavioral changes that stick, to include breaking destructive habits and establishing new patterns of effective coping that bring lasting change.
- Explore issues that may surround destructive worry—past abuse, depressive episodes, obsessive-compulsive disorder, attention deficit disorder, alcohol and drug abuse, and anxiety and personality disorders.
- Help the patient come to terms with past events that affect present thinking and behavior.
- Explore new life situations and social relationships.
- Help define and articulate problems, feelings, and issues arising from worry.

- Help identify major sources of stress and initiate actions to eliminate or reduce them.
- Identify and eliminate or reduce "triggers" for worry.
- Help deal with more than one illness. (For example, coping with anxiety alongside a diagnosis of cancer, recent heart problems, or alcohol and drug abuse. A patient cannot break the cycle of destructive worry while abusing alcohol or drugs.)
- Help create and recognize small successes in therapy that can be a foundation for future successes.
- Help prevent relapses into destructive worry, including helping the client monitor moods and mood swings.
- Be available to family members who are affected by a destructive worrier.
- Deal with stigmas that clients fear are attached to mental health problems.
- Help sort out the maze of questions regarding health insurance and psychological care.

It's important to recognize that over the past half-century many specialized forms of psychological therapy have been researched, developed, and applied to mental health issues. This is particularly true in treating destructive worry and anxiety. People seeking mental health care are not limited to classical psychoanalysis and in-depth psychology. Most therapists are not "purists" anyway, but include a number of different therapeutic methods tailored to the specific needs of the client. What follows is a discussion of these various therapeutic modalities.

Psychoanalytic Therapies

The grandfather of psychoanalysis is Sigmund Freud and his famous "talking cure." It has a reputation for being interminable (think Woody Allen). As developed by Freud and his disciples, classical psychoanalysis usually involves several therapy sessions a week over an extended period of time. This kind of therapy is based on the belief that current psychological problems are the result of repressed memories and feelings from the past. These repressed memories and feelings reside in the unconscious part of the mind and they surface into conscious life, creating psychological problems. This approach to therapy is more likely to be used when a person has a long history of destructive worry and anxiety and the causes for these persistent symptoms are not readily apparent. Psychoanalysis involves a client freely talking about past experiences, recalling painful events and the emotions associated with them. The psychoanalyst or therapist helps the client interpret and come to terms with his or her psychological history and problems. There are new psychoanalytic therapies that take less time than classic Freudian analysis.

Cognitive Therapy

This approach was developed in the 1960s and has proven remarkably helpful in treating destructive worry and anxiety. It is based on the understanding that destructive worry is experienced by people who have a distorted view of themselves and the world. Often, they feel negatively about themselves, their life experiences, and the future.

Cognitive therapy is designed to reshape negative thought patterns and maladaptive behavior. This does not mean promoting a falsely cheerful view of life; instead, the goal is to move a client from destructive worry to problem-solving. This therapeutic approach deals with the here and now of a person's life, addressing immediate problems to break recurring worry in a relatively short period of time. It also involves an educational process that helps clients to monitor their own thought patterns and to modify them.

Interpersonal Therapies

This approach to psychological treatment is based on the belief that destructive worry and anxiety are made worse by interpersonal problems in social relationships. It deals with unhappy relationships and the emotional stresses that accompany them. As with cognitive therapy, interpersonal therapy is directed at immediate problems and is designed to deal with symptoms in a relatively short period of time. Interpersonal therapies help the client with problems in social settings by developing coping mechanisms and social skills to repair or strengthen family ties, friendships, and working relationships. Clients are taught how to defuse confrontational situations with practical advice on what to say and do.

Behavioral Therapies

This therapy is an outgrowth of psychological behaviorism, a belief that our behaviors, emotions, moods, and reactions are learned and conditioned. Based on this theory, what we have "learned" can be "unlearned" and our "conditioned responses" can be "re-conditioned."

Some destructive behaviors (like drug abuse) are physiologically addictive. Others (like destructive worrying) are psychically habit-forming. Often, behaviors are both. Admittedly, behaviors that are central to a lifestyle are hard to change, but behavior therapy focuses on unlearning old dysfunctional behaviors and learning new and healthier behaviors. People can sometimes act their way into new ways of thinking more easily than they can think their way into new ways of acting; therefore, new behaviors can lead to new and healthier emotions. Treating destructive behavior treats destructive worry. Conversely, treating destructive worry treats destructive behavior.

Client-Centered Therapies

Carl Rogers was a pioneer in client-centered counseling, and this approach to therapy is sometimes called Rogerian. He emphasized that true and lasting change in a person's life comes about through "experience in a relationship." This therapy is grounded in the therapist's building a relationship of respect and understanding with the client. The therapist is non-directive and doesn't interpret psychological events or emotions or direct the client toward a certain action; instead, the therapist helps the client clarify feelings and thoughts and promotes a sense of self-esteem. Positive regard for the client is a hallmark of this approach, but that, of course, should be the hallmark of any therapy.

Group Therapies

Human beings are social creatures and spend most of their lives in various groups. Psychotherapy is often conducted with small groups. Various therapeutic modalities are used by the therapist to facilitate discussions in which individuals can learn coping and problem-solving skills. A group centered around a particular issue (alcoholism, spousal abuse, compulsive gambling, depression, destructive worry) serves as a means of powerful support. Group members deal with biases, stigmas, myths, fears, and shame. There is opportunity to confront accusations of weakness, laziness, and character defects. Groups are a safe place to find help, support, and hope. People learn that they are not alone.

Family Therapies

Family therapy is group therapy focused on the family and its individual members. Families and individuals don't get sick by themselves and they don't get well by themselves. When one member of the family has problems, it creates problems within the family. Family therapy can determine if a family member is carrying unacceptable emotional burdens for the entire family. It can enable family members to be both individuals and family members. It can define boundaries between family members, clarifying roles and functions, and allow all members to realize their full potential.

Finally, family therapies can foster equitable solutions to power imbalances within the family when a family member is excessively controlling.

Pastoral Counseling

This specialized form of counseling is done by ordained clergy with advanced training in pastoral psychotherapy. Pastoral counseling is unique because it combines psychotherapeutic methods with the healing resources of the Judeo-Christian tradition, allowing those involved to explore issues at the intersection of religion and mental health. Just as there are good and bad doctors, there is good and bad religion (and also good and bad pastoral counselors). Good religion and good pastoral counselors provide resources that are healing and foster a sense of hope. Their training focuses on dealing with people in crisis, combining the disciplines of theology, psychology, and the psycho-social sciences. Clergy who specialize in pastoral counseling have done post-seminary training and many have received a doctor of ministry degree with an emphasis in counseling.

Choosing a Therapist

Once destructive worriers realize that pervasive, overwhelming problems have taken control of their lives and they have decided to seek help, it's not always easy to know where to begin. To whom should I talk? Do I need to see a physician? Do I need to see a psychiatrist? Should I talk with a psychologist? Should I go see my pastor?

First, the destructive worrier needs to see a medical doctor. It can be a family physician or a generalist in internal medicine, but a thorough physical examination is necessary to establish that there are no medical illnesses present causing the symptoms of destructive worry. As we discussed earlier, there are many physical illnesses in which worry is a significant symptom. If none are found, the next step is some combination of medication, psychotherapy, counseling, and pastoral care, as appropriate. A well-designed treatment program helps educate and provides insight and support for successful therapy. Since medication and psychotherapy often go hand-in-hand, the following suggestions may help you begin the journey to wholeness and health. Begin with someone with whom you are already familiar and have some relationship. This might well be your family physician. Your physician already has some idea of your medical history and will be able to conduct a physical examination. Your physician will be able to prescribe medication, will be aware of medications you are currently taking, and will be able to refer you to other health professionals, including psychiatrists, psychologists, and pastoral counselors. A good pastor has some understanding of your life situation, your spiritual/emotional history, and your relationships. Your pastor should also be willing and able to refer you to other health professionals. You can also find qualified pastoral counseling through the following organizations:

- The American Association of Pastoral Counselors
- The Association of Clinical Pastoral Education
- The Canadian Association for Pastoral Practice and Education
- The College of Pastoral Supervision and Psychotherapy
- The Association of Professional Chaplains
- The National Association of Jewish Chaplains
- The National Institute of Business and Industrial Chaplains

When you first see a therapist, be sure you feel like you are in good hands. Ask questions concerning the therapist's training, background, approach to therapy, clinical experience, and the professional organizations to which he or she belongs. Explore the therapist's willingness to use a team approach to therapy (cooperating with any physician, psychiatrist, pastor, other counselor, and health professional you may also see) and ask what experience he or she has had in such a collaborative effort. Trust your intuition about whether you are able to talk with and form a good relationship with the therapist. Ask if the therapist recognizes biological and chemical origins of some symptoms of destructive worry and what his or her attitude is toward medication. Ask if the therapist is available to your family members, with your permission, to discuss non-confidential issues and questions regarding treatment, progress, needs, and goals. Ask what your therapy would entail and inquire about realistic goals and length of treatment. If at all possible, choose a therapist you don't see in other social settings, which might create embarrassment and conflicting boundary issues. Ask about costs, insurance, and other financial arrangements. If you don't feel comfortable with the responses, see another therapist. If you are still unsure of where to begin, telephone your state or county medical societies, your state or county psychological associations, or the organizations listed above for pastoral counselors. Any of these groups will have a referral line to provide you with a list of qualified professionals in your area. You need to find the right "fit" for you.

Perhaps the most important issue to be addressed in talk therapy is not the method of therapy, but the relationship between the therapist and the client. This involves the personalities of both parties, the perceived level of trust, and the success in forging a relationship. Studies of therapeutic relationships reveal that the most important factor in successful therapy is client motivation for change. The second is the therapist's personal attributes. A distant third is therapeutic modalities and technique. In other words, successful psychotherapy depends largely on a client's desire to get better and on the existence of good chemistry between the client and the therapist. Indeed, the client/therapist relationship may be the single most important curative factor in psychotherapy or counseling.

These descriptions are not meant to be exhaustive in their analysis of types of therapies and kinds of therapists in the tradition of Western medicine. Rather, they are intended to serve as a guide to help you in your search for medical, psychological, and pastoral support and treatment. Remember that as the patient, you are also the client and the consumer of services. It's important that your choice of a therapist and therapy fit your own sensitivities, needs, and treatment goals. The genuine test of psychological therapy is whether or not it works for you to further health and wholeness.

Chapter Eight

Managing Destructive Worry

Complementary and Alternative Therapy

"Those who fear the Lord will not be timid,
or play the coward, for he is their hope."

—Sirach 34:16

Richard down-shifted his '75 Mustang, lovingly restored with the help of his dad. He turned onto State Highway 182 and floor-boarded it. Maybe, he thought, I should just keep on going? The week before, his girlfriend had told him she might be pregnant. Only she really wasn't his girlfriend. She was more like a friend-girl. Friday night on Cemetery Road after a football game and with a six-pack between them. The last thing he wanted to do at age seventeen was get married. Especially to Sherry. But maybe she wasn't pregnant. He wasn't sure he could trust her to be straight with him. He was totally stressed out. Worried until he thought he would puke. And he felt really guilty.

He agreed it wasn't right to have sex before marriage. And he knew he shouldn't have been drinking. That wasn't right either.

Both illegal and immoral. He hadn't talked to his dad. It would just kill him. He had talked to his preacher. Yeah, he was bad. Prayer didn't help the guilt or get him out of the trouble he was in. Richard pulled to the side of the road. He was there a half hour later when a highway patrol car pulled up behind him. He showed his identification and said he was just thinking. He waited while the officer ran the information on his computer, then admonished him to drive carefully. After he was gone, Richard made a U-turn and started back home.

Guilt and worry together are a toxic combination. Either emotion sucks the life out of a person, and in synergy, they can create a downward spiral that is hard to reverse.

Complementary and Alternative Therapy methods may be grouped broadly under two headings: alternative care and general health improvement. Therapies under the CAT umbrella include, but are not limited to, acupuncture, yoga, bio-feedback, meditation, relaxation techniques, aromatherapy, massage, herbal treatments, tai chi, homeopathy, naturopathy, and dance therapy. Other treatment concepts appear at regular intervals, and all have been used to treat destructive worry and anxiety, as well as identifiable and diagnosable mental illness. There is little doubt that many of these treatments are safe and effective ways to make an individual feel better.

For instance, surrounding a person with pleasant scents improves mood, at least temporarily. Keeping pets, if one is so inclined, is good for people. It gives them companionship and something to care for. The beneficial effects of touch are well-documented. Yoga reduces stress and improves physical conditioning and flexibility. Concentrated "breath work" is an integral part of yoga and can also be practiced by itself, and it appears to improve depression, anxiety, and panic attacks. Traditional Chinese medicine posits that good health depends on the life force *(qi,* pronounced "chee") flowing harmoniously among the elements of wood, fire, earth, metal, and water; the pathogenic factors of cold, wind, dryness, heat, dampness, and fire; and the emotions of joy, anger, anxiety, obsession, sadness, horror, and fear. This kind of language appeals to certain temperaments because the language, both profound but unfathomable, cites concrete elements and emotions and has the force of a mystical religion.

Assess

Returning to our SOAP analysis, let us assess CAT options in managing destructive worry. Western medicine begins with the bias that anything not proven by the scientific method is speculative. We know that therapy sometimes works just because people believe it will (through the power of suggestion, or mind over matter). Western medicines that go through formal review are tested in double-blind studies using drugs and placebos, and in every one, a percentage of patients on the placebo get better. In evaluating CATs, success in treating diseases with herbal remedies has often been measured by testimonials and success stories—in other words, anecdotal evidence. Sound research to identify the active ingredient, establish correct dosage, and monitor for side effects has generally not been done. Yet it's important to note that like Western medicine, CAT is big business, and it's almost impossible to change an industry (think automobile). Medical doctors have been surprised by studies that found that consumers spend almost as much annually on CAT as they do on Western medicine (without the benefit of insurance) and that more patients seek out CAT therapists than visit MDs.

There are many reasons people seek complementary and alternative therapies. Medical doctors sometimes seem more interested in laboratory tests and technical procedures than the patient.

Western medicine has extended the normal life span, but longer life is not synonymous with wholeness and health. And then, Western medical science has been unable to successfully treat many chronic and recurrent diseases, and patients will go to almost any length to find relief from their diseases.

On the other hand, Western medical science has several reservations about complementary and alternative therapies. CATs generally aren't undergirded by a unified theory, nor are they coordinated in any manner. CATs are not usually evaluated for objective, reproducible, proven results. Very few herbs have been subjected to controlled, random, double-blind studies (in which neither the patient nor the researcher knows who is receiving the drug or the placebo). Such studies are now taking place in various centers, but clinical trials take time. CATs usually aren't integrated in any manner, and the patient remains alone through the course of treatment. Solitary treatment is not ideal therapy for destructive worry and anxiety.

Patients have choices in therapy, and they are exercising that right, but common sense is required to avoid falling for every trendy treatment.

Patients should be knowledgeable about alternative choices and use good judgment. We should all make ourselves familiar with the risks. Guard against extravagant claims, especially testimonials. Remember that herbs and supplements are not regulated by the Food and Drug Administration; consequently, purity and dosage may vary in the manufacturing process. Herbs that have pharmacological activity have side effects, cause allergic reactions, and are toxic, just like prescription medications. *Ginkgo biloba* has anticoagulant properties that may cause bleeding (strokes, bowel hemorrhage, or bleeding during surgery). Soy contains natural estrogens, and there is concern it might have adverse effects in women with potential for breast or uterine cancer. The active ingredient in *ma huang* is ephedrine, and it can cause dangerous elevations in blood pressure. St. John's wort has some effect on serotonin, norepinephrine, and dopamine—molecules implicated in depression, obsessive compulsive disorder, destructive worry, and anxiety—but controlled studies have failed to document actual clinical improvement in these mental health problems. SAMe (S-adenosylmethionine) is the new rage for treating depression, liver disease, and osteoarthritis. It appears to boost the activity of the neurotransmitters dopamine and serotonin, but it is not clear how clinically useful it is in dealing with depression, destructive worry, or anxiety. SAMe may cause mania when taken by a person who is bipolar.

When patients visit medical doctors they sometimes don't tell their physician what herbs and supplements they are taking, either because they don't think of them as "medicines" or because they are embarrassed to admit they have sought alternative therapies. Tell your doctor everything you take and do to improve your health.

People should guard against unscrupulous practitioners in any area of medicine. Remember P. T. Barnum's aphorism, "It's a sin not to take a sucker's money," and regard all therapeutic claims with a healthy skepticism.

Plan

Destructive worry affects all aspects of living. We believe that ideal treatment is a collaborative effort that combines the skills of various therapists using the tools from their several disciplines. If there are biological causes for worry and anxiety (whether medical or mental illnesses), they must be addressed with medication and ancillary medical therapies. For the mental health problems associated with destructive worry and anxiety, psychotherapy is helpful.

A new kind of medicine is emerging called integrative medicine, which incorporates Western medicine, CAT, and spiritual insight. It may utilize medication, psychological therapies, relaxation techniques, yoga, meditation, and, for those religiously inclined, spiritual discipline and prayer. The idea is to bring healers together, drawing on each discipline's individual strengths. The key word is discipline, indicating that the approach in all of these fields of endeavor must be thorough, reflective, studious, and rigorous. Think clearly, reflect honestly, and integrate wisely. At the heart of integrative medicine is a focus on overall health improvement. Start taking better care of yourself. Therapy involves lifestyle changes that are fundamental to well-being. Eat right, get plenty of sleep, avoid substance abuse, and begin an exercise program.

First, practice good nutrition. Don't you hate it when your mother was right? Medical science has known for almost three centuries that certain nutrients are vital in preventing specific diseases. (For example, vitamin C deficiency produces a disease called scurvy, while vitamin D deficiency produces a disease called rickets.) But for the past seventy-five years, medicine has been entranced by the tricks it could perform. And prodigious feats they were—the repair of birth defects, open-heart surgery, brain surgery, organ transplants, cancer therapy, endoscopy, replacement body parts!

Studies in nutrition are just now catching up with advances in techniques. We are slowly unraveling the hitherto mysterious interplay of many nutrients in our food supply. Antioxidants (such as vitamin E and A and beta-carotene), free radicals, SAM-e, folic acid, omega-3 fatty acids, and co-enzyme Q10 promote heart health and brain health and may improve depression, while cholesterol adversely affects the heart and circulatory system. Diets should be low in saturated fats and trans-fats, and should contain generous proportions of fruits, vegetables, whole grains, fish, nuts, and flaxseed oil. Boring, right? It's easier to take a supplement than eat vegetables. Interestingly, there is no good evidence that taking vitamins and supplements in pill form works as well as consuming the same in natural foods. Beyond the pure science of nutrition, good food in good company is a healing experience of body, mind, and spirit that can best be described under the heading of table fellowship (a spiritual discipline).

The restorative power of sleep, although not fully understood, has been known since antiquity. Get a good night's sleep. We neglect this simple step to good health at our peril. Again, Mom was right!

Avoid the detrimental effects on health of smoking and substance abuse. The association of cancer and cardiovascular disease with tobacco use is well known. Caffeine (chocolate, tea, and coffee), when taken in large amounts and close to bedtime, cause disturbed sleep patterns. Alcohol is a sedative, a depressant. It may make the worried, anxious, or depressed individual feel better temporarily, but it interferes with thinking, judgment, and sleep. It reduces inhibitions and contributes to antisocial behavior. Don't be a loner. Remember, human contact contributes to health and well-being.

Good health is impossible without regular exercise. *Any* type of exercise releases endorphins that boost neurotransmitters and affect both the mind and body, improving both mental and physical health. Exercise improves bone density, regulates blood sugar, promotes cardiovascular health, and reduces tension, frustration, anger, aggression, worry, and anxiety. Exercise enhances the overall sense of well-being, improves disturbed sleep patterns, elevates mood, and promotes clear thinking and concentration. Remember, the value of human interaction applies to exercise, too. Choose an enjoyable and communal activity like dance, jazzercise, or a team sport. Exercising with others lends social support, elevates mood, and focuses the mind. Take walks alone certainly, but also in the company of a friend or relative.

Therapy will never solve all of a person's problems, because problems are a part of living. A person without problems or worries or anxiety isn't engaged in life or has no life of substance. Even

Sigmund Freud felt that the goal of psychoanalysis was to turn neurotic misery into everyday suffering. That may sound pessimistic, but to move beyond neurosis to having choices and options is no small thing. Most people with destructive worry and anxiety will improve with proper therapy. Treatment should be continued for whatever length of time is necessary. Like other illnesses, destructive worry and anxiety can be nagging and chronic, and times of therapy may be needed throughout the person's life. People may need evaluation and "tune-ups," just like an arthritis or high blood pressure patient might. Chronic, destructive worriers, in the context of their support systems, must cooperate with health care professionals in treatment plans. Doctors call this patient compliance. In the treatment of destructive habits as well as disease, failure often occurs simply because the patient doesn't follow through with the prescribed program of therapy.

It remains to be said that good health is not perfect health. Alleviating destructive worry and anxiety does not create the perfect mood. But there is hope for such persons, their families, friends, and coworkers. There are so many modalities of therapy to alleviate destructive worry and anxiety that the harmful effects of these problems need not be suffered. Get help! Free yourself! Choose life!

Chapter Nine

ANXIETY AND RELIGION

The Humanity of Longing

"The only thing that is truly able to disarm the sophistry of sin is faith, courage to believe . . ., courage to renounce anxiety without anxiety, which only faith can do; faith does not thereby annihilate anxiety, but itself eternally young, it extricates itself from anxiety's moment of death. Only faith is able to do this, for only in faith is the synthesis eternal and at every moment possible."

—Soren Kierkegaard, *The Concept of Anxiety*

Martha's family of origin was very close-knit. They had moved several times during Martha's childhood, including a move overseas when she was a teenager. She entered university overseas and was beginning her studies when the rest of her family moved back to the United States, leaving Martha with enormous sadness, uncertainty, loneliness, stress, and anger.

In the years since this event, Martha lives with a constant fear that she will be left alone and that she cannot trust relationships.

She has recurring panic about being separated from her husband or losing close friends. She works overtime at trying to control people and situations to ensure that she will not be left alone, all the while knowing that this is a fruitless waste of energy. Yet when panic ensues, she is reduced to uncontrollable tears, begging, and occasional violent reactions. She becomes clingy and resents any time others spend away from her. Filled with simultaneous anger and sadness, she becomes depressed and ruminates on "not being good enough" for people to stay with her.

Martha is suffering from separation anxiety disorder. While separation anxiety happens commonly among children afraid of leaving their parents (to go to school, to stay overnight at a friend's house), it can also recur and persist in adulthood. It is often associated with depression and/or other anxiety disorders such as panic disorder.

Religion is one of the great human endeavors, ranked alongside science, medicine, law, the arts, architecture, exploration, and soldiering. These vocations have been essential to civilization's long march through history. In fact, anxiety, the hardwired core of human nature, is the stimulus that gave momentum to these essential vocations. Their common objective is to broaden the human experience and stave off death.

At bottom, the human race is anxious about death. Death, grinning in the wings of civilization, reaches toward us with a skeletal hand. Humankind's one great, shared, invigorating gift is life. We think and move and feel and breathe. That all stops with death. Death may take us suddenly and unaware. Or death may gradually squeeze the life out of us in a long, agonizing, painful, progressive loss of mind and functions. We not only lose life, our humanity is debased. When death comes, we pass from warm flesh to cold clay in that instant. We know this, and furthermore we have the capacity to anticipate it. This is not an abstraction. It's not a theory. It's not a philosophical musing. The one, solid, basic human reality is that death is the end of life. There are some who say, "Fine! Let it come! So what?" But most of us feel that disquieting seed of regret that ripens into anxiety and fear. We want to know the answer to "So what?" And this is a religious question.

The world religions offer insight into the human condition, but it has been a rough road. Jonathan Swift once remarked that most people have only enough religion to make them hate, but not enough to make them love. We have only to look at recorded history to see the truth of his observation. Jews, Muslims, Hindus, Shintos, Sikhs, Buddhists, and Christians have been at war with each other from the foundations of their individual cultures. Further, the sub-sects of these great world religions have also been at each other's throats in fratricidal warfare. To paraphrase Swift, it may also be true that we have only enough religion to make us anxious, but not enough to make us secure. We all are stuck with the dilemma that we can't live with anxiety and we can't live without it.

We, the authors of this book, approach the dilemma of anxiety from the Christian tradition. Jesus taught, "Be not anxious." Two apostolic pillars of the Church picked up this theme. St. John wrote, "Perfect love casts out fear," linking love and courage. St. Paul, a late-comer to the apostolic band, commends "faith, hope and love" as last-ing virtues, and suggests they are antidotes to fear and anxiety. But how, and in what way, do these dictums address our anxious core?

At the center of spirituality is a longing for what is absent. It is an ache, like homesickness. To have longing is to be religious. To have longing is also to be anxious. We anxiously long for a sense of wholeness, meaning, and security. And we hope for the fulfillment of our heart's longings. Too often, purveyors of Christianity have cast hope only as a future fulfillment in heaven. The Bible speaks of something beyond. But it also points us toward something now. The truly spiritual and religious choose a full life now.

Our anxious biology and religious longing are similar and yet in tension, the one impelling us to preserve our selves and the other urging us to embrace possibilities beyond our selves. We fear life, death, and God. We face the same question Shakespeare spoke through Hamlet: "To be or not to be?" We make this choice—being and not being, life and death—in a thousand practical ways every day. It is in those moments that we either "choose life" or "accept death." Anxiety, in its various forms, can prevent us from making active choices, but not choosing is the stuff of death. Paralysis steals away our freedom, diminishes our courage, subverts our future, and robs us of joy. Choosing frees us and gives us courage to embark on a future with all of its possibilities, including both risk and joy. At each of those moments, we touch the very core of our humanity. We come to our central concerns as human beings. We address the spiritual nature of our existence.

The first stories of the Bible in the book of Genesis are about our becoming human. The primal story of Eden is a story of both living in Paradise and losing Paradise. Man and Woman, created in the image of God, know innocence and unity with God. This is Paradise. Man and Woman have vocations and freedom. They eat of the tree of knowledge. The wisdom gained is human awareness ("self-consciousness"). They fall into time. They are not only alive, but they *know* that they are alive. They are conscious of their existence. This knowledge is accompanied by bitter dread. Two things happen. They know they are naked and vulnerable. And they know they shall die. They are Something now, but they will become Nothing. Formerly intimate with God, the source of their being, they now are driven from their deity's presence. They lose Paradise. They are fully free and face a creative but challenging existence. Life outside Paradise is hard, and they are now responsible for themselves. They are anxious—and humankind has been so ever since.

The story of Adam and Eve is a universal story, but it is also local. It is our story, and we know it is our story. Soren Kierkegaard spent a lifetime addressing the reality that human existence is filled with anxiety. He believed anxiety is fundamentally a religious question. Redemption in the midst of anxiety means a leap of faith into life. Human beings are made anxious because of threats. There are physical threats: falling off the ladder. There are emotional threats: losing a job. But equally significant, human beings churn up anxiety from within. Just being human sets us on a journey of anxious steps, one after the other. Kierkegaard says that every human being embarks on an adventure to learn to be anxious in the proper way. He believes we will perish if we have never known anxiety, but that we will meet the same fate if we succumb to anxiety. When we learn to use anxiety constructively, it can become our teacher at the deepest level of our human existence. Healthy fear can impart wisdom and be a signpost to courage. In fact, life-giving fear may be the only real cure for being afraid. Dealing with anxiety is the key to spiritual growth and human maturation.

We are creatures of spiritual nostalgia. We long to find the source of our existence, and we long to fulfill our present existence. We are people of memory and of hope. These human characteristics mean we are people of anxiety. How can we understand the relationship between our humanity and our religion, between anxiety and hope, between memory and yearning, between worry and worship, between fear and faith? How can we overcome our loneliness and separation? We must probe the chaos and messiness of our own lives to address our deepest religious questions.

Jesus and Anxiety

Christians begin their reflection on anxiety and religion with Jesus. The Christian faith is centered in the incarnation, the embodiment of God in the human Jesus. It is about Jesus of Nazareth in a specific setting—Judea in the first century when Herod was King. Jesus is not a divine being floating in mid-air between heaven and earth. He is not a celestial shadow of a god untouched by human experience and immune from human suffering. He is not half God, half man. But in a sacred, mysterious manner, he is God as man. Fully God and fully human. We understand this in accordance with historic and orthodox Christian faith, which has clung to the full humanity of Jesus in spite of the church's misguided inclinations throughout history to spiritualize him, outfit him in the respectable clothing of the scientific age, or clean up his act. Martin Luther's earthy description is a pertinent reminder: Jesus came as an "earthworm in the feedbox of a donkey." At the heart of Christian faith is the understanding of the incarnation—Jesus, fleshly and sensuous, but a true and faithful expression of God. The emphasis in the gospel is on the humanity of God rather than the deity of Jesus. Jesus, the first-century Galilean, who loved and trusted and wept and hungered. Who knew loneliness and fear and suffering and worrisome anxiety. Who struggled with temptation and erupted in anger. Who was "made to be sin." Who was tempted in every way as we are tempted. Who knew the experience of unanswered prayer and unrequited love. Who knew some things but didn't know others. Who could do some things and couldn't do others. Who grappled with human limitations. Who sought the meaning and experience of freedom. Who remembered, experienced, and hoped. Who knew abandonment and God-forsakenness. Who experienced the approach of certain death. Who endured death under the most dreadful circumstances. We turn, with eyes of faith, to this brother and companion, our fellow human being, to address our experience of anxiety.

Rethinking Jesus

Jesus was a prophet, not a spiritual Pollyanna. He spoke of the power of faith, not the power of positive thinking. He was a realist, not a romantic. He concerned himself with wisdom in living, not wish-fulfillment. His piety engaged the world, with no hint of a world-escaping dream or a world-denying nightmare. He loved the same world that God loved. He hoped for the future of God's own making, what he called in his teaching "the coming of the Kingdom of God."

As a prophetic, realistic, wisdom-filled, faith-centered, and hope-oriented human being, a lover and teacher who called for abundant life, he knew the world was dangerous. In his last discourses in the Gospel of John, he tells the disciples, "In this world you will have tribulation." In the German Bible the phrase is translated, "In this world you have angst." This is our word for anxiety. Jesus knew that life in this world (which he loved with the heart of God) was filled with fear and uncertainty. With angst. Angst literally means a narrowing of the breathing passages. Angst threatens the "breath of life" that God breathed into our nostrils in the beginning. Jesus's realism gives an authentic picture of the nature of anxiety and a clear acknowledgment of this as part of what it means to be a human being. In one of his parables, he pictures the "word of life" being "choked by the cares of this world."

Not only did Jesus tell his disciples they would experience angst, he acknowledges his own anxiety. As he is facing the journey that will take him to his death, he simply says, "Now is my soul troubled." Fear of abandonment and separation from God is embedded in Jesus's anxious Gethsemane prayer and Golgotha cry of God-forsakenness.

We emphasize the view of the world held by Jesus because it stands in stark contrast to so much popular religion today, which presents Jesus as a purveyor of happiness, comfort, and wealth.

People talk about the "Be-happy-attitudes." His words are transformed into rules for a happy, whiz-bang, carefree life. Or they are sold as a secret code to be mastered to change anxiety into self-fulfillment. We can almost imagine Alfred E. Newman sitting on the side of the mountain grinning inanely and saying, "What, me worry?" This cheap trick reduces the power of the beatitudes and Jesus's beatific vision of a kingdom-centered life. The care-filled life of the suffering servant becomes the carefree life of the happy-go-lucky Christian. The incarnational Good News of the gospel becomes a shoddy formula for selfish fulfillment. The gospel is tilted toward glory, success, and wealth. In happy-go-lucky Christianity, the anxiety that is at the heart of the human experience is not addressed, but dismissed. Surface happiness is promoted rather than the possibility of becoming a person before God in the very depths of our being. We don't genuinely confront the angst Jesus said his disciples would have in this world, because a happy, bobble-head Jesus can never meet us at such depths.

Such lives must be lived on the surface because we bury our fear that the gospel is impotent to reach us down where the monster lives. The ticking time-bomb of this dread makes us anxious. When the gospel of suffering, surrender, and service is exchanged for a gospel of happiness, we have given up not only the only hope of confronting the monster of anxiety but the only genuine hope for attending to the fear of God. When we avoid and deny our anxiety, we avoid and deny our humanity. We exchange the fully lived life in the kingdom, with its freedom and responsibility, for Christian escapism. Which, by the way, is not Christian, nor does it truly escape anything.

Jesus acknowledges that anxiety accompanies the human journey, his and ours. He directly confronts the monster, and calls us to a life in which anxiety is named, addressed, and denied supremacy. The anxiety that prevents abundant life by paralyzing us with fear is defanged by a faith that releases, frees, and empowers us. The anxiety that chokes us is overcome by the hope that helps us breathe. Jesus's vision of life is one in which we are challenged to live through anxiety rather than deny it, attempt to escape it, or be defeated by it. This timeless virtue empowers us with the courage to act freely, move forward in hope, and reach out to fellow sojourners.

This is a mystery. A great paradox. How can the ferocious, debilitating anxiety, which is part of our humanity, be tamed? In the very text in John's Gospel where Jesus says we will have anxiety in this world, he makes this promise to his disciples: "I have said this to you, that in me you may have peace."

What is the peace of Christ? Well, since we will have anxiety, this peace is surely not the absence of challenge, struggle, trouble, and fear. Christ was not immune to these aspects of life. Why would his followers be? To be without anxiety is to be without our humanity. Getting rid of anxiety is neither a possible nor an appropriate goal for human beings. The peace of Christ and the core values of faith, hope, and love don't allow us to escape life or death.

Destructive anxiety attacks us in four ways. First, anxiety attacks us with meaninglessness. We fear a journey to nothingness, life seems to go empty at its core. Second, anxiety attacks us with alienation. Life is not trustworthy because we feel God-forsaken— separated from the source of our being. Third, anxiety attacks us with loneliness. We fear separation from people important to us, from dependable relationships, from a common community, and at our deepest level, a cosmic separation from the heartbeat of the universe. Fourth, anxiety attacks us with hopelessness. We fear there is no future and that life must be lived without hope.

In overcoming these attacks, the peace of Christ is not centered in *peace of mind,* but in the *peace of God.* It is "kingdom peace," the peace that belongs to Christ's vision of life. That vision is presented in the Gospels in various ways—the parables, the Sermon on the Mount, and so on—but it is anchored in the concept of a relationship. The dynamics of a life lived in relationships are focused in faith, hope, and love. The goal for kingdom people is the freedom to live through anxiety by means of a faith that reaches out in loving relationships and hopeful actions. Freedom is not simply an idea. Freedom is an act.

The "irresistible impossibility," a term coined by Robert Frost about the Sermon on the Mount, is exemplified in Jesus's summons, "Do not be anxious." This is not some sweet-Jesus piece of impractical advice, but a statement about whether we will be *dominated* by anxiety or *empowered* by trust. It's about a life oriented by trust in God. The context is God's faithfulness and care. "Be not anxious" is an invitation to trust one's life to God rather than a command to conquer one's own anxiety by trying very hard.

This takes us to the heart of the Christian vision of life. We cannot save ourselves. We are not just out of kilter, needing to fine-tune our gyroscope. We are broken and isolated, alienated and divided, and separated from the origin and foundation of our being, which is God. At this basic level of Christian faith, we don't need simply repair, but redemption. We not only need healing, but salvation. In the gospel story, this redemption is seen as liberation—freedom that comes from outside our own selves. It's called grace. Without grace from beyond ourselves, we cannot be freed to live with anxiety and through anxiety to a future. Otherwise, we remain isolated in our pride, alienated by self-contempt and consumed with self-concern. Reinhold Niebuhr explains this by saying a person can be "so concerned about himself that he cannot release himself for the adventure of love." Jesus's vision for disciples in the "kingdom life" is to trust a caring God who places anxiety and fear in proper proportion in the midst of life and its uncertainties. Kingdom people are freed to realize wholeness in faith, hope, and love.

Jurgen Moltmann, whose theology is anchored in the biblical vision of hope, beautifully portrays the relationship between anxiety, freedom, and hope. To paraphrase Moltmann, the whole of life is an adventure, a great risk, clinging to hope in the face of continual anxiety. The journey along life's troubled road to the future is the road to freedom. For Moltmann, anxiety and hope are the two sides of the coin of freedom. Grasp the coin of freedom and you grasp anxiety. Stick the coin of freedom in your pocket and you pocket hope. One cannot have freedom without anxiety. One cannot have freedom without hope. They are inextricably linked. If you desire freedom, be prepared for anxiety. If you choose freedom, be prepared to hope. The road to freedom is paved with anxiety and signposted by hope.

The question remains, in the midst of debilitating worry, overpowering fear, and paralyzing anxiety, how do we find new beginnings and the courage to walk through the "iron gates of life" on the freedom road for the adventure of love? How do we break the chains of poisonous, life-denying anxiety so we can experience life-affirming courage and love-fulfilling freedom? It begins by reframing our religious understandings in three areas—religion and realism, religion and reinterpretation, and religion and redemption. We will turn to these areas in the next chapter.

Chapter Ten

REFRAMING RELIGIOUS UNDERSTANDING

Finding New Beginnings

"We would rather be ruined than changed.
We would rather die in our dread than climb the
cross of the moment and let our illusions die."

—W. H. Auden

William had grown up in a conservative religious home in a small town in the South. His life was circumscribed by clear and certain religious doctrines, a keen ethical sense of a black-and-white personal morality, and a worldview shaped by a sense of being born into the right race, right nationality, and right church. In fact, this "uniqueness of rightness" pervaded his worldview. The task in life was to keep the rules in an ordered and certain world, work hard, and successfully engage in his profession, his church and its evangelism programs, and his family life. He was bright, committed, and respected. He continued to work within a worldview that God was in his heaven and rewarded the efforts of the morally pure, the religiously correct, and those with a Protestant work ethic. He continued to live and work within a context that shared these convictions. There was no room in this world for the "ambiguity of reality."

In mid-life, he left the circumscribed environment of his childhood years and early adult life. He became a business consultant in a multinational corporation and moved with his growing family to a large major city. He successfully engaged in the corporate world and its expectations. But soon severe anxieties began to manifest themselves as he confronted radically different worldviews, a plurality of religious environments and perspectives, and a world of complexity with regard to a clash of values in ethical decisions and behaviors. He experienced a widening gulf between his lived experience and his prescribed religious faith. Certainty began to disappear while "commitment to his various certainties" grew stronger. Within this very real clash, anxiety increased and induced a psychological paralysis that kept him from moving forward in dealing with the challenges of his life and context. The only solution he could imagine was returning to his old worldview, but that perspective no longer made sense to him. He was facing a crisis of faith and experience, leading to disappointment, bewilderment, and conflict.

As we noted in the introduction to this book, all people have a religious outlook on life, even if that outlook is claimed to be non-religious. Any system of belief by which we order our lives is a religion, and it doesn't have to use God-talk. What we believe about our religion affects our general outlook on life. In fact, religious beliefs, for most of us, are a mixed bag. Religion is not necessarily a good or a bad thing, helpful or troubling, healthy or unhealthy. From the Christian perspective, much of the Bible is about the effects of both "good" and "bad" religion.

Anxiety, as we have said over and over again, is part of our humanity. At its core, it is both biological (our hardwired amygdala) and existential (spiritual/religious longing). And just as anxiety can become distorted into psychological or medical disease, it can also find religious expression—or in some cases, religion itself can become sick. With this in mind, it is important to begin our discussion of the Christian religion by reframing our religious questions. Some modern philosophers have cast religion as "the opiate of the people" (Marx), an illusion (Freud), or a mere sociological construct (Durkheim). While it has been and can be all of these things, it should be both more and qualitatively different for the disciples of Jesus. To borrow Tillich's phrase, religion holds and expresses our ultimate concerns regarding life, its vulnerability and uncertainty, our brief existence and certain death.

Isaiah spoke in powerful prophetic language of God's saving activity in the world of someone to come who would be called Wonderful Counselor, mighty God, everlasting Father, and the Prince of Peace. Christians have used this vision as a description of Jesus's cosmic significance. The Gospels tell of Jesus's humanity and how he encountered the challenges of life and death. He spoke and acted truthfully, realistically, compassionately, and wisely. He had a passion for living, loved his traveling companions, even at their worst, and enjoyed table fellowship. He trusted God and retained hope for the future, even in the face of his own acknowledged anxiety and dread.

The practice of the Christian faith is set in a narrow, person-specific, historical context of a life lived in human relationships with human limitations, at a given time and place. Disciples of Jesus acknowledge these origins as the setting for all conversations that frame Christian faith. These origins are the basis for a realistic life lived in meaning and connectedness in this natural world. They are the foundation for facing the future with hope. Disregard for these Christian realities sets disciples adrift in a religion of fantasy and denial. Whatever that may be as a philosophy, it is not the Christian religion, which belongs to the realm of faith, hope, and love. Christian life is lived in freedom with imagination, creativity, and courage. In faith, risk must be taken. Love must be expressed with passionate and compassionate energy in *agape, philia,* and *eros*—caring love, brotherly/sisterly love, and erotic love. Hope must be expressed by engaging in life in ways that fully expect that our desire for peace and well-being (what the Hebrew Bible calls *shalom)* will one day be realized. The deepest yearnings of our hearts and reality will one day be harmonized.

Religion and Reinterpretation

Christian faith has both content (what is believed) and a dynamic (the living, breathing process by which beliefs are formulated and expressed on the journey). Christian faith's content is centered in the person of Jesus. The faith dynamic is located in historically conditioned texts, interpretations over two thousand years, and our own life experiences. Faith and its practice is not a static, unchanging code; growth and maturation continue. Faith comes when our story meets the biblical story at some crossroad in our lives, for we must interpret such an event and make sense of it within the broader experiences of our lives. We call this conversion. In the process of conversion, we reinterpret our past journeys, our present experiences, and our future hopes in light of a new story. Our stories and our identities change. The intersection of our stories and the biblical story and our interpretation of it is a continual process.

Sometimes we become locked into a warped faith system or misguided interpretation that is inappropriate, life-denying, and paralyzing. This is especially true in relationship to the ways we experience anxiety, thus robbing us of the joy of life and the freedom to actually live. Anxiety becomes a prison rather than a teacher, a spiritual disability rather than a spiritual opportunity to exercise the courage to become our true selves before God.

Continual reinterpretation of our experiences is critical if we are to exercise our freedom to break out of our prisons of anxiety. The future is open only to those with a hopeful vision and the courage to take the road. We understand our lives, our journeys, and our relationships by the meaning we give to all of the events of our personal histories. Interpreting and reinterpreting our personal stories give us a means of dealing with our pasts and preparing for the future. Interpreting and reinterpreting the religious faith that shapes our actions is likewise important. It is especially important to encounter afresh our views of God, our basic outlooks on life, and the ways in which we see our own selves. The importance of continual reinterpretation, especially our views of God, is laid out clearly by Jurgen Moltmann in *The Experiment Hope*:

> Without a revolution in the concept of God, however, there will be no revolutionary faith. Without God's liberation from idolatrous images produced by anxiety and *hubris* [pride], there will be no liberating theology . . . . Behind the . . . crisis of the church in modern society stands . . . the question of God . . . Which God governs Christian existence—the one who was crucified or the idols of religion, class, race, and society?

With this in mind we turn our attention to certain views of God.

Views of God.
Just over fifty years ago (about the same time that W. H. Auden published "The Age of Anxiety"), the Anglican priest J. B. Phillips wrote a small book entitled *Your God Is Too Small*. In this insightful book, he explored images of God that he believed were inadequate to address the challenges and threats of modern society and scientific

thought. He explored such common images as God as Resident Policeman, Parental Hangover, Absolute Perfection, Managing Director, Perennial Grievance, and others. He argued that distorted images of God leave people feeling helpless in a threatening world. This sense of vulnerability is a common source of anxiety. The connection between views of God and debilitating anxiety has become increasingly clear and has been discussed in both psychoanalytical and theological literature over the past half-century.

For example, pastoral theologian Seward Hiltner and psychiatrist Karl Menninger, writing in the 1960s, quoted an anonymous source as saying, "Tell me the nature of the god a man believes in or denies, and I will tell you how he rears his children, deals with his neighbor, expresses his sexual impulses, and contributes to peace or war." We have seen this observation become reality in the current distorted practices of religious terrorism, whether perpetrated by Christians, Jews, or Muslims. Religious faith has direct consequences for the attitudes and actions expressed in our lives. We might also say, "Tell me the nature of the god a person believes in or denies, and we can begin to discern the nature and results of his or her anxiety."

Likewise, Viktor Frankl, M.D., Ph.D., and a professor of neurology and psychiatry, interprets neurotic anxiety as a way of existence. He uses such terms as "spiritual attitudes," "spiritual deficits," "spiritual rebirth," and "uneasiness of the spirit." He connects neurotic anxiety to the anxiety that is part of being human, in which spiritual issues become expressed in physical symptoms and/or phobias focused in various organs of the body.

Much of the Jewish and Christian tradition revealed in the Bible is concerned with false images, distorted understandings, and debilitating views of God. The Bible stories show how faith impacts personal life and the life of the community. We turn to a powerful parable of Jesus to illustrate how our image of God influences our lives and abilities to act in the face of anxiety. Jesus tells a story of three people who respectively receive five talents, two talents, and one talent from their master when he goes away on a trip. The person with the five talents invests the money and multiplies them to ten talents to give to the master upon his return. Likewise, the person with the two talents multiplies them to four talents to give to the master. But the story turns on the person with the one talent who simply buried the money in order to give it back to the master when he returned. The people who used and multiplied their talents are commended. The person who buried the talent is condemned.

The story is a means of conversation about the nature of the self, life gifts, and what a person does with them and why. It reveals something of unused energy and capacity. It is risky to invest one's self and one's gifts in a dangerous world. All three people reacted to the challenge and the risk. Two faced the challenge and took the risk. The third retreated from the challenge and avoided the risk. Why? Two reasons emerge in the story. One reason was the view the one-talent person held of the master. The master is perceived as a "hard man." The other reason was the one-talent person's view of himself: "I was afraid." The first reason is projected outward on to the master. The second reason is internalized.

From a religious perspective, both our views of God and our views of our selves are critical in addressing paralyzing anxiety. We may view God as a deity of hard righteousness and severe judgment, void of compassion and impossible to please. This same view can be applied to lives and our relationships. If we view ourselves as the one-talent man did, we don't think of ourselves as bad, wasteful, or irresponsible people. We view ourselves as scrupulous people, fearful and paralyzed by anxiety. George Arthur Buttrick, the great Presbyterian preacher, and Walter Wink, the New Testament scholar of "transformational Bible study" methods, see in this parable both a failure of courage and a failure of imagination. The talents in the parable don't symbolize money or even giftedness, but rather the whole self, especially our undeveloped potential and inferior qualities. If we adopt the view of the one-talent person, our insignificant "whole, complete self" cannot imagine being worthy of a life-gift, nor can we imagine how to engage it usefully. Our fear and lack of imagination forecast failure. We will not measure up or be good enough.

The two people who had the courage and imagination to use their talents had a view of the master that contrasted sharply to the view of the person who buried the talent. They viewed the master as one who expected them to use their talents—their life-gifts—by engaging in the risk of life. The receipt of the life-gift was an invitation to invest in life, to live and to risk. This is quite different from the person who viewed the master in terms of reward and punishment. Often our religious focus is on reward and punishment, heaven and hell, rather than on God and life. Our religious "attention" needs to be refocused. This requires reinterpretation. The disciple who views God as a deity who gives life and *also* issues a summons for courageous risk receives life eternal. The disciple who views God as a hard master who weighs us severely on his scales of justice for reward and punishment, finds torment, weeping, and the outer darkness of paralyzing anxiety.

Views of Self

There is a powerful connection between our views of God and the views we hold of our selves. Ludwig Feuerbach, a German theologian, said, "Consciousness of God is self-consciousness, knowledge of God is self-knowledge . . . Religion is the solemn unveiling of a man's hidden treasures, the revelation of his intimate thoughts, the open confession of his love-secrets." Or, as Rubem Alves, a Latin American theologian said, "The study of religion, therefore, far from being a window that opens only on panoramic vistas, is a mirror in which we see ourselves. . . Religion is closer to our personal experience than we wish to admit." Reinterpreting our view of God involves reinterpreting our view of our selves. We can view our selves in isolation, but a true vision of our selves is always in our relationship to others and to our life task. In this context, faith is dynamic and ongoing. It is a conversation with God, not a settled mathematical formula. Again, it is a process, not a product in the religious marketplace.

If our view of God is always in terms of a power broker or sheer "almightiness," we never see God's love, vulnerability, and suffering. Then when we sense our powerlessness, we see ourselves as victims before the mysteries and vicissitudes of life. As in the parable, "we are afraid." If this is our basic understanding of ourselves, we allow our fearful anxieties to control us rather than responding with courageous imagination to manage life's anxieties.

Views of Life

In the same way that our views of God affect our view of our selves, our views of God and our selves affect our views of life. Do we experience life as fundamentally "against" us or as " with us"? To be sure, injuries, threats, disappointments, failures, and betrayals are part of life. Remember, "In this world you will have troubles." The question is whether we approach the ocean of life as a dangerous and inevitable place to drown or a dangerous but exhilarating place to swim. For all of us, if we dig deep enough, the reason for paralyzing anxiety is the experience of betrayal. A trust gone bad. Faith in human nature was destroyed by someone held dear and trustworthy. Life is no longer safe. This view can be the result of a monstrous injustice such as the Holocaust or the smaller heartbreak of being betrayed by a friend. Whatever it is, the lesson is ingrained as a constant warning: "Be careful, people cannot be counted on. Life is unjust. Nothing is worth the risk." But if we choose avoidance, a narrow and fearful life is the result.

Religion is about views of God, views of self, and views of life. Religion is cast in concepts of faith (imagination and anxiety), hope (a future), and love (courage to trust). Before addressing these concepts, we must examine our understanding of religion and redemption.

Religion and Redemption

What question about human existence, meaning, and destiny does religion seek to answer? The first question we must ask is, "What is the fundamental problem confronting us as human beings?" We said earlier in this chapter that in the Christian vision of life, we cannot save ourselves. We need more than repair; we need redemption. We need more than healing; we need salvation. This is what the Christian doctrine of redemption is about. Just as "theology matters" in terms of our fundamental view of God, ourselves, and life, so "theologies of atonement" matter in the way we understand redemption. What do human beings need to be "saved from" and "saved for"? How does this relate to the fundamental human question of anxiety before life and death?

Paul Tillich said humans suffer from three types of anxiety. First, there is anxiety caused by issues of fate and death. What is our destiny? Second, there is anxiety caused by the experience of guilt and condemnation. Are we good enough? Third, there is anxiety caused by emptiness or meaninglessness. Do we count? According to Tillich, we are threatened with the anxiety of death, the anxiety of condemnation, and the anxiety of meaninglessness. In all three forms, anxiety is simply part of being human (philosophers call this "ontological" anxiety). It is a normal part of life. But anxiety can expand and become an abnormal part of life. These are religious issues addressed by the Christian doctrine of atonement.

There are three major theories of atonement based on Christ's suffering and death. Douglas John Hall, Tillich's student and now a professor of theology, discusses and correlates Tillich's "types of anxiety" with the "theories of atonement." There is the theory explained by the concept of rescue and deliverance. There is the theory explained by the concept of sacrifice. And there is the theory explained by the concept of revelation. Each theory of atonement is drawn from a different concept of the human predicament. The idea of rescue and deliverance can be correlated with Tillich's anxiety of fate and death. This was the predominant anxiety of the Mediterranean world of early Christianity. Atonement theories characterized by sacrifice can be correlated with Tillich's anxiety of guilt and condemnation. This was the predominant anxiety of medieval society and the early Reformation. Atonement theories centered in revelation can be correlated with Tillich's anxiety of meaninglessness. This is the anxiety of the modern and postmodern eras.

The point is, again, that whatever "question" humankind wanted to solve with Christian theology, the "answer" they found in the doctrine of atonement (redemption and salvation) was shaped by their historical time. The history of intellectual thought regarding the human predicament shapes Christian theology. Just as important, our individual stories shape our personal faith when understanding the atonement.

Our goal is not to discuss the strengths and weaknesses of each theory of atonement, nor to cherry-pick from all three theories, but to show how our personal religion can be applied to our personal experience of debilitating anxiety. In this manner, we may find the creative courage to invest our life-gift in productive living. In order to do this, each one of us must articulate our fundamental religious question. What do you, Dear Reader (to steal a stylistic phrase from the Gothic novel), think your predicament is in your life before God?

Is God angry with you?
What is your worth?

Are you good enough?

What do you need to be saved from?

What do you need to be saved for?

What is the role of fear in your life and in your experience of religion?

What are you afraid of?

What does God require of you?

What do you require of God?

Are you concerned with reward and punishment in the afterlife?

Do you suffer a sense of guilt?

Do you suffer a sense of shame?

Do you experience life fatalistically?

Are you free?

How free are you?

What is your purpose in life?

Does your life have meaning?

Does it seem pointless?

What is your fundamental principle in life?

What do you expect from life?

What do you want to give life?

These and related questions will help you name your understanding of the human predicament.

If your basic understanding of your predicament is one of oppression, bondage, or being trapped—where the sinful condition is understood as being enslaved to Fate and Death (realities stronger than you are)—then atonement may be understood from the early Christian perspective as rescue and deliverance. You want to be free. Free from what? Well, free from sin and death. Free from cultural bondage. Free from the "principalities and powers" of this world. Free from the threat of evil. Free from social embarrassment.

Free from selfish preoccupation. And much more. These are fundamental, legitimate concerns of just being a human being. The classical theory of the atonement is that Jesus Christ came to rescue and deliver us. He "ransomed us" and set us free.

If your basic understanding of your predicament is that you are a sinner, guilty before the righteousness and justice of God, and you are afraid because you know you stand condemned, then atonement may be understood along the lines of the early Reformation in which Jesus provides the sacrifice for your sins. God, in Jesus Christ, the perfect human being, steps in for you and takes your sins upon himself by his sacrificial death. This sacrificial theory of atonement answers the question of how we as guilty and condemned human beings can be made right with a deity who cannot "overlook" sin.

If your understanding of your predicament is that you are a finite human being in a vast and unfathomable universe, and you are left with fearful uncertainty and meaninglessness, then atonement may be understood along the lines of revelation and demonstration. In this theory of atonement, the cross of Jesus is not so much "rescue" or "sacrifice," but a revelation and demonstration that we are loved by God. As you become aware in "your moment" that you are truly God's beloved, you are transformed into a lover of God, lover of yourself, and lover of others. Being loved and loving addresses Tillich's anxiety of meaninglessness and despair, and correlates with the human predicament as interpreted by modern and postmodern cultures.

These theories of atonement remain in the church's tradition to help us attend to the anxiety—our fundamental religious questions—that belongs to the human condition. The redemptive work of Christ, the meaning of the cross, and the suffering love of God can sustain us as we confront anxiety in all of its forms. There are always more questions to be asked and mysteries of divine love to be fathomed. Faith is, indeed, the great staff we grasp to support us as we stride along life's pathway. Staff in hand, we pay attention to the questions that haunt us. Faith, hope, and love are God's gifts that empower us for courageous engagement with life. These three abiding Christian virtues address our anxiety, as well as each time zone of our lives—past, present, and future. Faith attends to the anxiety of guilt and condemnation and gives us a story for dealing with our past. Hope attends to the anxiety of fate and death and gives us a story to open our lives to our future. Love attends to the anxiety of meaninglessness and despair and gives us a vocation (a life-task coupled with our life-gift) to infuse our present with purpose and meaning. Faith restores, hope relieves, and love heals the wounds of anxiety.

We would like to commend three practical ways to attend to anxiety from the perspective of Christianity. They are based in the concepts of religion and a living, realistic faith. They are not simply concepts to think about, but actions to take. They are choices open to us. They are decisions growing out of our understanding of God, life, and self. They are convictions concerning our salvation, which we believe means becoming our whole selves before God. They are also centered in the gospel of love that Jesus proclaimed and lived. Jesus's parable of "The Good Samaritan" ends with the challenge, "Go, and do likewise." Freedom to confront anxiety and move through it to life is an act that frees us. "Doing likewise" takes the courage to risk, a commitment to a life task, and connections to a community.

Chapter Eleven

FINDING FREEDOM

The Courage to Take Risks

"Anxiety is the dizziness of freedom."
—Soren Kierkegaard, *The Concept of Dread*

Max was bright, funny, and well-liked. He was also afraid most of the time. He covered this fear with dismissive humor. But as time went by, playing the clown wore thin. He wasn't afraid of anything or anyone or any situation specifically, but he perceived the world as a dangerous place, lacking dependability and reliability. Life could not be trusted. Something would surely always go wrong. Not only did he have difficulty in trusting "life in general," but this sense began to extend to people. Whatever Max did, he did well, but he never saw it that way. Sticking with something, completing something, or staying on course for the long haul became increasingly difficult. Max became the walking voice of the writer of Ecclesiastes—all seemed vanity: "I looked on all the works my hands had wrought. And on the labor that I had labored to do; and behold, all was vanity and a vexation of the spirit. . . . Therefore, I went about to cause my heart to despair" (Eccles. 2:11, 20 KJV). Most of the time, Max's free-floating anxiety had no focal point outside himself; in some cases, he found ever-shifting focal points. He became the "wind watcher" and "cloud observer" of Ecclesiastes, paralyzed into "never sowing or reaping." (Eccles. 11:4). Eventually, life simply became worry about worry, anxiety about anxiety. He could never relax. The worry machine cranked relentlessly on. There seemed to be no "off" switch.

The foundation for all virtues is courage. It is the cornerstone in the building of character. Courage is both the starting point and the stuff that holds everything else together. Courage gives substance to our ideals, values, beliefs, and desires. Debilitating anxiety is the failure of courage. We cower before the threats and vicissitudes of life. Dread overwhelms us. William Sloan Coffin, in reflecting on "the courage to love," argues that the point of the gospel involves the courage to take risks. God takes risks in the incarnation, in becoming human in Jesus. Jesus takes risks in his ministry. Courage is not the absence of fear. Courage is a decision to take the risk, even in the face of uncertainties. Misgivings may be intellectual, moral, or physical, and feed into the uncertainties of living. Coffin says our choice is to be "scared to death" or "brought to life." Our fear of death is connected to our fear of life. Many people, according to Coffin, fear the "cure" more than the illness. They prefer paralysis to freedom. The courage to be well and whole is a crucial virtue. In Greek thought, *arete* (virtue) carries within it the attribute of courage. Courage was understood as an ethical concept because without it, we are unable to act. If we are unable to act, we cannot be effective. Courage is a virtue that combines both the technique and the art of living well.

How do we find the courage to risk when fear is our basic problem? How do we act when we are paralyzed? We must begin by looking at the nature of the fear that paralyzes us. If we follow our shadow, we trace the facsimile of our self back to the light that illuminates our real self. Spiritual director and Episcopal priest Robert C. Morris says that "learning the art of life-giving fear may be the only cure for being afraid." This is reminiscent of William Sloan Coffin's view that "the only security in life lies in embracing our insecurities." What is the difference between life-giving fear and life-denying fear?

The Hebrew Bible distinguishes between kinds of fear. Understanding these distinctions is helpful. *Yare*—fear—is to hold in reverence and awe. *Cur, dechal,* and *yagor*—fear—is to be physically afraid or to be filled with dread. All of these Hebrew words can be used to speak of the "fear of God," but the word used most commonly is *yare*. In Hebrew thought, as well as in other philosophies down through the centuries, being afraid sucks the life out of us. It leaves us weak, paralyzed, and powerless. Awe, on the other hand, leaves us apprehensive and aware that we stand in need, hat in hand. Awe is a critical, realistic, and, at bottom, spiritual trait. This holy fear is a life-saving grace. Accepting that we stand in need before the mystery of God and the vicissitudes of life can free us to recognize that although we are not all-powerful, we are still powerful—not omnipotent, but potent.

If our fundamental view of God is omnipotence ("a hard man"), rather than vulnerable love, then in wanting to be like God we desire omnipotence ourselves. Experience teaches us we are not. Faith and hope show us that we can be like God when empowered with the vulnerable love of God. There is freedom in this knowledge. The Garden story prevented us from becoming omnipotent. Cast out of the Garden, we were filled with terrifying and life-denying paralysis. Our desire to "be God" robs us of the power and courage to become who we are as human beings. God is God and we are humans. We are to live our lives before God with holy awe, drawing on the graces of faith, hope, and love to empower us. This approaches the central truth of the wisdom literature of the Hebrew Bible. We find in Psalms, "The fear of the Lord is the beginning of wisdom"; in Proverbs we read, "The knowledge of the Holy One is insight." We the authors argue that the "fear of the Lord and knowledge of the Holy One" is also the beginning of courage.

Why is this so? Because Psalms and Proverbs—in the setting for the verses quoted—enumerate the blessings awaiting the person who acquires the wisdom-getting awe-of-God. In Psalm 112, such persons are happy, blessed, enduring, gracious, merciful, just, generous, steadfast, unafraid, secure, steady, victorious, and compassionate. In Proverbs 8, such persons are prudent, intelligent, truthful, straightforward, understanding, discrete, good, humble, insightful, strong, loving, and searching. The result of courageous wisdom is that if we fear God we will fear nothing else, though contrastingly, if we don't fear God we will fear everything else. We must recognize the difference between holy fear (which is awe before the mystery of God) and paralyzing fear (which is incapacitating dread). When we do, we arrive at Jesus's teaching on the love of God, neighbor, and self. The Christian response to anxiety is the power of vulnerable love that gives us the courage to live because it frees us from the prison of a self that fears everything.

Tucked away near the end of the New Testament is a little book in which the apostolic writer reflects on Christian faith in terms of life and love. The book was not written in a time of safety. Christians were experiencing some of the trouble Jesus predicted. The writer of John says,

And so we know and rely on the love God has for us.

God is love. Whoever lives in love lives in God, and God in him. In this way, love is made complete among us so that we will have confidence on the day of judgment, because in this world we are like him. There is no fear in love. But perfect love drives out fear, because fear has to do with punishment. The one who fears is not made perfect in love.

We love because he first loved us. (1 John 4:16–19)

In this Christian vision, God is the source of love. This echoes our discussion of the atonement in which we recognize that we cannot save ourselves. God, not human romanticism, goodwill, or the progressive human spirit, is the source of love. This is so because, according to the text just quoted, God is love. God is not to be understood in the Greek sense of an abstract principle, but in the Judeo-Christian sense that, as Fred Craddock, the gifted preacher says, "all the acts of God through and in history have been directed toward our ultimate well-being." This is a vital insight in understanding the fear of God as the beginning of both wisdom and courage. It is an equally important insight to understand that our capacity to love is derived from God. We love because we have been loved.

Love casts out fear because we are no longer terrified of punishment. The Good News of the gospel is that the love of God who is "for us, not against us" addresses our core, biologically wired anxiety as well as our mundane anxiety. We remain aware of our vulnerability to the hard edges of the world, but a greater truth enfolds our lives—the fearful and wonderful care of God who, in Jesus Christ, frees us from anxiety with the courage to love. The loving God who is "for us and not against us" graciously extends forgiveness through Jesus Christ. This is why Tillich says, "Forgiveness is . . . the divine answer, to the question implied in our existence." Of course, Tillich reminds us that an "answer is an answer only for . . .

the person . . . who . . . is aware of the question." The Christian view of the love of God is seen most clearly in the sufferings of Jesus, not in the Greek concept of God's omnipotence.

Jürgen Moltmann, a German theologian, asks the question, "What is religiously integrated anxiety?" His answer centers on release from anxiety through Christ's "earthly and most profoundly human suffering and fear," not through the divine omnipotence of a heavenly Christ. "Blessed anxiety," in Moltmann's terms, is "anxiety that has been liberated." Dietrich Bonhoeffer, one of the German pastors who suffered at the hands of the Nazis, wrote from his prison cell shortly before he was hanged, "Only the suffering God can help us."

God graces us with bold courage to love in the day of judgment. What is the day of judgment? It is not only the biblical references to judgment day at the end of earthly history (although this is important), but any day in which we face a crisis (which is, after all, the Greek word for judgment). Bold courage to love in a day of crisis is not bravado from summoning up personal heroics, but courage based on reverential awe in faith. Love that gives up self-interest cuts the ground from under fear. Giving up our self-interest is not a craven submission to God—another form of tyranny—but a faithful surrender to God. We enter a relationship of empowering trust. Oh, but can we do this? No. God can, but we are an imperfect instrument. In our life's walk and work there are loose ends. Life is not orderly. Life is messy. This paradox of fear and love, anxiety and courage was captured memorably long ago in two powerful lines of a beloved hymn, "Amazing Grace": *'Twas grace that taught my heart to fear, And grace my fears relieved.*

Commitment to Our Life Tasks

Developing the courage to risk precedes the next step we must take in order to move through paralyzing anxiety to the art of living.

Courage to become our true selves is to find our life-tasks and become committed to them. Our life-tasks are not just our jobs, although those are included. A life-task is a vocation that is centered on a purpose larger than our selves and our self-concerns. Having a life-task is not the same thing as having goals, although goals provide orientation—planning, discipline, and the work necessary to achieve them. Yet goals themselves can be completely self-centered, and as such, they can produce more anxiety. A life-task is the "why," the purpose and meaning, of your life. A passionate mission in life carries us through anxiety. A "why" for living can bear almost any "how" in the process of living. Understanding, choosing, and engaging in a life-task makes it easier to cast off destructive anxiety. Broadly speaking, and drawing on biblical language, our life-task is to "love God, neighbor, and self." Identifying and engaging in our life-task with singular purpose is what Soren Kierkegaard called "purity of heart." Commitment to our life-task is part of our becoming who we desire to become as human beings. Life apart from a life-task is meaningless. We turn away from anxiety by turning to our life-task.

When we embark on our unique and singular life-task, we address both the destructive anxiety and the mundane anxiety of living. This allows us to live the journey, going through our anxiety. We don't avoid it or deny it. We courageously take the risk and engage our anxiety with faith, hope, and love. Only then can we be at peace. Spiritually, people suffering from destructive anxiety live with a spiritual deficit. They can't engage in life. They are unable to become what they want to become and do what they want to do. But rather than getting rid of anxiety so they can get on with life, they must do the opposite. They must follow the spirit and message of the gospel and stand life on its head. They get on with life *in order to* reduce their anxiety.

Engaging in our life-task is a critical step in overcoming destructive anxiety. To actually become our selves before God, rather than wrestling with anxiety and focusing on our selves, it is paramount that we embark on a task that involves a purpose greater than our selves. The task, as well as the self, is discovered in community.

Connecting to Community

Our most basic anxieties are often fear of abandonment, not being accepted, not measuring up, not being good enough, social embarrassment, and failure. These fears often isolate us, and this compounds our problems, because isolation increases our anxiety and fear. It heightens our feelings that we are powerless. We not only need the courage to engage in our life-task, but we need the courage to reach out and connect with people. We need meaningful community. Without it, we cannot expect to find wholeness and health. We need to form good relationships if we are to break out of this cycle of anxiety and isolation that only leads to more anxiety and isolation. Good relationships must be both loving and creative. Carl Rogers, the psychotherapist, emphasized that people do not "get well" through something they are taught but through changes that come in relationships. Genuine connections with people are key to good mental and emotional health. Relationships are the best antidote to the ravages of anxiety. The road to good mental health can't be traveled alone.

The Judeo-Christian faith has always been anchored in a connection to the community. The Christian faith is a relational faith, not a system of beliefs or a philosophical tradition. It is a personal faith connected to a Person, Jesus Christ. It is not a solitary faith, but is connected to people. Jesus's kingdom vision was one in which people would "weep with those who weep and rejoice with those who rejoice." The earliest Jerusalem church was noted for its fellowship of love and communal life. Saint Basil believed "individualism" was a violation of the law of love. He taught that no one can realize the will of God for himself or herself when the person separates himself/herself from the fate of others. Bishop Alexander cites Saint Basil as saying, "Every indifference to the fate of other men, and every kind of individualism . . . was not only profoundly depraved, but also self-destructive in its nature." Martin Luther, a man haunted by anxiety, confronted it through his connection to the sacramental fellowship of Christian community. Quoting Luther in this regard:

> If anyone is in despair, if he be distressed by his sinful con-science or terrified by death, or have any other burden on his heart and desire to be rid of them all, let him go joyfully to the sacrament of the altar and lay down his grief in the midst of the congregation and seek help from the entire company of the spiritual body.... The immeasurable grace and mercy of God are given us in this sacrament that we may there lay down all misery and tribulation [angst/anxi-ety] and put it on the congregation and especially on Christ, and may joyfully strengthen and comfort ourselves and say: "Though I am a sinner and have fallen, though this or that misfortune has befallen me, I will go to the sacrament to receive a sign from God that I have on my side Christ's righteousness, life and sufferings . . . ."

In Christian faith, the fellowship of the church community is not some afterthought of the gospel, but is an essential part of it. The church is not simply a place for socializing but is a sacramental gift of the Holy Spirit. It is grace that is seen because it is acted upon in relationships in a community that shares a common life whose source is God. Life in this community is always and forever felt, seen, and expressed in relationships. It is God-centered and God-empowered. T. S. Eliot captured this vision poetically in "Choruses from the Rock":

What Life have you if you have not life together?
There is no life that is not lived in community,
And no community not lived in the praise of God.

Seeking out a community addresses one of the fundamental spiritual needs of the human being—the need to be your self in relationship to God. It addresses the "local" anxiety we feel from the isolated loneliness in our individual lives. But it also addresses the "cosmic" anxiety we feel from the isolated loneliness of living in a vast, almost unfathomable universe where we are specks on a solitary spinning planet. To paraphrase Charles Stinnette, who linked theology and psychiatry, the Christian answer to anxiety is framed in terms of faith within a loving community. The most profound example is seen in the New Testament communities where the sick were healed, the mourners were comforted, and the poor were nurtured. Faith involves more than a set of creedal beliefs. Faith springs from our unreserved participation in the faith community to which we are committed—in life and death—into the hands of God. This relationship of trust is our source of courage to accept with honesty our own predicament, and yet to live by faith.

Traditionally, one of the functions of the church has been to break the self-centered cycle of isolation by bringing individuals into a creative, loving community. Wayne Oates, the well-known professor of the psychology of religion, says, "This drive toward community transforms anxiety into social feeling . . . and converts egocentric anxieties . . . into a fellowship of concern for other people." He explains that the purpose of the gospel is to release us *from* the self-centered anxieties of sin; *from* the petty, puny systems of a legalistic way of life; and *from* calloused insensitivity to genuine ethical realities of living. At the same time, the gospel releases us *to* a concern for the welfare of others; *to* preference of another before our selves; and *to* the adoration of the Lord Jesus Christ. When we have been set free from the bondage of fear, we can genuinely give our selves without reservation to the needs of others.

We must commit to the notion that we become whole not in isolation but through ongoing recovery in community. Mutual care occurs when we each give what we have to give, and receive what we need to receive. This is Christian fellowship. Unfortunately, much American Christianity is focused on personal salvation, personal success, and personal happiness, rather than the well-being of all of God's people and all of God's creation. The church desperately needs to be confronted with realism, reinterpretation, and redemption in The Way of the vulnerable, serving, and suffering Lord of the church. Ironically, it may be those suffering from the loneliness and alienation of anxiety who, in their common need, will find each other in a true community and will reclaim the church and its authentic healing role in culture.

Chapter Twelve

BECOMING OURSELVES

Non-Anxious Worry and Liberated Living

"The need is to lead people in their concrete existence to their unique and singular task of life. It was up to her to become what she was going to be . . . and as long as she had not become that she could not be at peace. The anxiety crisis needs to be reshaped into a spiritual rebirth."

—Victor Frankl, *The Doctor of the Soul*

J ack, a decorated Vietnam War veteran who was wounded when his position was overrun by the North Vietnamese in a night attack, had suffered clinical depression for years. His depression had been alleviated by antidepressant medication and cognitive behavioral therapy. The need for talk therapy had diminished through the years, and he functioned reasonably well on antidepressants alone. Jack, now in his sixties, began to be afraid at night, especially when alone. This was a significant problem because he and his wife had lived in separate cities for a decade due to the demands of their jobs.

Jack found it necessary to check the doors to his home several times each night before he went to bed to confirm that they were locked. He also purchased tamper-proof door-blockers to secure the outside doors from forced entry. He slept fitfully. The slightest noise inside or outside his house awakened him. He would jolt awake, heart pounding, pulse racing, straining to sort out the night noises. He feared that intruders had slipped into his home. He considered buying a handgun for protection, but his psychiatrist dissuaded him. Jack possessed a Russian carbine that he had picked up after an engagement with the North Vietnamese Army in 1966. He had welded the breach shut for safety when he returned from Vietnam, but he retrieved the deactivated weapon from storage. He locked the bayonet into position beneath the muzzle and placed the carbine on the floor beside his bed at night. On occasion, his night terror became so great that he got up and, holding the weapon for a bayonet thrust, made his way through the darkened house, making sure that he was secure.

Jack's night terrors did not occur, or were much less severe, when his wife was home with him. He also felt more secure in his second home, in which he lived in an attached condominium within a gated and walled community. During those nights he felt he had a "secure perimeter." Along with his night terrors, he began to have more frequent and vivid nightmares of Vietnam.

Jack had post-traumatic stress disorder. This is a specific clinical presentation of anxiety that may also accompany depression. An element of obsessive-compulsive disorder had also crept into his behavior, as manifested by his repetitious checking of outside doors at night to be certain they were locked.

*ᵉ   *ᵉ   *ᵉ

We have argued in this book that worry and anxiety belong to life but that life should not belong to worry and anxiety. Worry and anxiety should not be your master. Worry can be your servant.

Anxiety can be your teacher. But neither needs to be your curse, your prison, your demon, your permanent address, or the slaughterhouse of your future.

This is not because anxiety and worry will disappear. They will not. The goal is not exorcism, but disempowerment. It is not banishment, but freedom through engagement. In the same way that courage is not the lack of fear but victory over fear—through a decision to act—attending to anxiety doesn't cause anxiety to disappear, but allows victory over its paralyzing and destructive power.

The scale of worry runs something like this:

Life-threatening (either through physical death or the inability to live fully)	Pathological/ Diseased	Inappropriate and destructive	Appropriate but unhelpful	Appropriate and helpful

Attention to our own experiences, conversations with significant others, and education about worry and anxiety (such as the material in this book) helps us locate ourselves somewhere along this scale. This helps determine if our responses to anxiety are effective.

Destructive worry is disproportionate to the threat that causes us to be anxious. A line in a T. S. Eliot poem refers to "measuring out our lives in coffee spoons." Such a life is marked by timidity, indecisiveness, and caution. In the end, a person who lives this way has only haunting memories of unfulfilled aspirations. On the other hand, appropriate worry is a proper response to the threat that causes us to be anxious. We recognize and encounter potential threats. We name them and relieve our anxiety by moving through with appropriate action.

Seeking Professional Help

As discussed earlier, depending where we are on the scale, any of us may seek support in the minister's study, the physician's clinic, or the psychiatrist's or counselor's office. Two indications for seeking professional help are the intensity of anxiety and its duration. If the intensity of worry and anxiety is such that it diminishes your life, blocks social interaction, paralyzes your ability to act, or is so compulsively present that it drains joy from your life, professional help should be sought. Also, if worry and anxiety lasts for days or is constantly recurring, professional help should be sought.

Focusing on Life

Fundamentally, the issue that is important for all of us is life—life that, in Jesus's teaching, is called abundant life. The focus is not anxiety. The focus is life, and this is a crucial distinction. We argued earlier that we need to reframe our understanding and interpretations of God, ourselves, and life. Unless we do this, we will not be free from our demons of anxiety, galvanized beyond paralytic worry, and released from our prison of fear. The first and most fundamental insight in reframing our approach to anxiety is this: *We do not get rid of anxiety in order to get on with life; we get on with life in order to move through anxiety.*

The central spiritual issue that confronts us as Christians is this: What is the word that gives life? That heals, frees, forgives, and raises the dead? That word is grace. The all-encompassing reality of grace, spoken by the Deity at the heart of the universe. This gracing love—from beyond our own power, achievement, brokenness, and sin—is the God of living relationships who is for us. It is in this relationship that we find life. While nature, fate, and circumstance are indifferent to us, God is not. Through grace and its offspring—faith, love, and hope—we find the courage to become ourselves before God. In the process of becoming ourselves before God, we overcome our anxiety.

Approaching Anxiety and Worry

We approach life's anxiety and worry in three ways. The first approach is to avoid confronting anxiety. The result is paralysis, and it robs us of life. The second approach is to deny anxiety. This approach is foolish and dangerous. We walk through life with false bravado. The third approach is to have the grace to use anxiety constructively. Kierkegaard thought if we could learn to be anxious in the right way, we had learned the most important thing. Through this approach, we are empowered to be our selves before God, to freely risk for the future, to connect with others in the giving and receiving of love, and to embark on the adventure of finding our life-task. We have turned from fear of the world to the fear of God—a life touched by awe, reverence, and humility before the great mystery of life. This is the beginning of wisdom. Courage is not another tyranny. It is a release from the tyranny of anxiety's death grip on our life that kills creativity and the freedom to act. The Bible calls this freedom from sin and death. In Jesus's words, we are now free to be "in the world but not of the world." We are free to be engaged in the world, but not dominated by the world. The yearning of hope embraces an open future.

The final work of grace in our lives is to make us gracious in our living—liberated from destructive anxiety and pure self-concern. Thus armed, there are some steps we can take along the way to "invest our talents" and plunge forward into liberated living.

Taking Steps toward Freedom

There are practical things we can do to respond to God's gracious word of life, acts of freedom that break the chains of destructive worry. In these final pages, let's review some of the key ideas to be sure they stay fresh in our minds.

Confront

The first step is facing our anxiety. Fight-or-flight is our instinctive response to any threat, real or imagined. By confronting anxiety we avoid the ostrich syndrome—the head-in-the-sand approach to challenges—and we make ourselves aware that there are both external and internal aspects to anxiety. Situations producing external anxiety can be addressed. We cannot run away from internal anxiety. We can never outrun our problems if they are within us. Consciously and purposefully confronting anxiety and moving through it has a cumulative positive effect in dealing with anxiety. In confronting anxiety we can name our fears, and by naming them, we take a reality check. Are our worries real or imagined? Are they set in the present or the future?

Clarify

A sense of chaos accompanies anxiety. The mind races. Thoughts spin out of control. We must slow the mind down and aim for clarity. We must SOAP the situation. What are the Subjective elements? What is happening inside me? What do I feel? What is the Objective threat, problem, or cause of worry? What is happening around me? Assess the situation and trace the source. Relate the subjective and objective dimensions of the worry. Make a Plan. Is the problem or threat solvable? How do I go about addressing it? What help or support do I need? Where or from whom can I find it? Break the problem down into parts. Analyze the parts and their relation to the whole. Part of the clarifying process is to change the language and our fundamental ways of thinking about the problem. We cannot resolve issues of anxiety by using the same language and the same way of thinking that we used when we were allowing anxiety to control us. Remember the adage: "If we always do what we've always done, we'll always get what we've always gotten." The following statement, widely attributed to Mahatma Gandhi, expresses things more poetically and powerfully: "Your beliefs become your thoughts. Your thoughts become your words. Your words become your actions. Your actions become your habits. Your habits become your values. Your values become your destiny."

Connect

Worry isolates. We feel both a personal loneliness and a cosmic loneliness. As the Lamentations say in the Bible, "Is it nothing to you, all you who pass by? Is there any sorrow like mine?" Or in the Psalmist's words: "I am the scorn of my adversaries, a horror to my neighbors, an object of dread to my acquaintances; those who see me in the street flee from me." We do not want to be with others and feel others do not want to be with us. Truth to tell, we are not too fond of our own company! Yet we stay home alone, we brood alone, we drink alone. We basically cut ourselves off at the very time we need to connect! We disappear into a self-made prison or drift into a self-imposed exile. We need to make every effort to fight this tendency toward isolation and to make connections. All Twelve Step groups recognize the danger of isolation and have developed a system of "sponsors" to provide companionship and connection. What are some of the connections available to us?

Family

Without attention, all things fall apart! Buildings, cars, and gardens. Institutions, organizations, and communities. The body, the mind, and the spirit. Marriages, families, and relationships. Everything falls apart without care.

We recognize that not all people live in families, and that families and marriages are often wounded and filled with anxiety. Still, connection with family, if it is possible, is a key connection. Make time to be with family in eating, conversation, play, worship, and common interests. Proximity is not connection, and taking family life for granted does not nurture these relationships. Talk and listen, interact, touch, hug, and support each other. The family, together, should take care of the past, live in the present, and look to the future.

Friends

Friendship is a powerful antidote to loneliness and isolation. It is also an antidote to family claustrophobia and isolation. Making and nurturing friendships should be a priority. The proverb is true: "Friends multiply our joys and divide our sorrows." One or two very close friends is important. Openness, camaraderie, the sharing of stories, laughter, concerns, problems, and stresses with a close friend breaks self-centered isolation and reduces the "me-against-the-world" syndrome. Friendship defuses self-contempt, self-pity, self-hatred, self-recrimination, and the loneliness of self-imposed exile. Make a friend. Spend time with the friend. The give-and-take of friendship feeds the rhythm of gracious living.

Faith Community

Connection with a local faith community places one in a structured context of care and support. It is a place to belong and to hear one's name pronounced with acceptance. It is a place to participate in worthwhile matters. It is a place to be needed. We not only receive, but we also give to a cause larger than our selves. A faith community also provides connection to history, tradition, ritual, study, and reflection. It is a place where individual stories are told and listened to in tandem with the stories of sacred texts and sacred journeys—the faith and life struggles of others through the ages. It is a place of worship—songs, prayers, and sacraments. It connects us to mystery, awe, reverence, and celebration. Without dimensions of worship in our lives, our whole selves shrivel. The individual human spirit and inner spiritual strength are nurtured in such communities.

Faith Source

A central claim of the Christian faith is that the "reality of being" at the heart of the universe, God, has a human face. The basic affirmation of the Bible is that the God revealed, experienced, and reflected on in Holy Scripture is the God who utters the word of grace, the God who is "for us" and makes the journey with us. God not only speaks, but also listens. The faith journey is an invitation to conversation. Prayer and meditation are means of connection. The personal connection we make through faith in God gives life a transcendent reference point. One gift of daily prayer is that it brings a freeing rhythm of recognition and connection into our lives. The structure of prayer is confession, gratitude, and intercession.

Confession has two aspects: confessing our faith and confessing our sin, brokenness, and need. Confession of faith is an act of praise, lifting our eyes beyond the horizons of our little lives to God. Confession of sin, brokenness, and need is an act of acknowledgment. We name our demons and seek forgiveness, healing, and acceptance. We give up our claims to omnipotence and righteous perfection. We also hand over our feelings of worthlessness and alienation.

Gratitude in prayer serves as a powerful reminder that we are blessed, the recipients of grace. To live without thanksgiving is to live without grace. Gratitude is an antidote to self-pity. Intercession, or prayer for others who need divine care and support, lifts our eyes beyond our selves and beyond our self-obsession. Others have needs, and often their need is us! Intercessory prayer, paradoxically, pays attention not only to the needs of others but to our own need to be needed.

Connection to God through faith moves us beyond the mundane and trivial of our lives to the sacred and the spiritual. Albert Einstein, the father of modern physics, often expressed his profound respect for both the mystery of the sacred dimension of human existence and the complexities of the physical universe. One observation of his that has graced posters, coffee mugs, bookmarks, and more is this lovely insight: "Either everything is a miracle or nothing is a miracle." His preference for the former understanding is quite clear.

Connection to God, the source of grace, asks the "forgiveness" question. We pointed out earlier that Tillich said this was *the* question of human existence. Connection to God provides the "forgiveness" answer. The conviction we, the authors, have drawn from life experience, as well as over eighty years of medical and pastoral practice, is that no sane person is so obtuse, shallow, out of touch, and self-centered that they don't know, in their heart of hearts, that they need forgiveness. We want release, but we will not "let go." As long as we won't let go, we actually "bind" ourselves. Frederick Buechner pointed out in his observations on Frank Baum's *The Wizard of Oz* that the lion wanted courage, the tin man wanted a heart, and the scarecrow wanted a brain. What the wizard helped them see is that they already had what they wanted. And they each exercised their courage, their hearts, and their brains when faced with threat and anxiety. Connection to the source of faith helps us recognize that we have been graced with the gifts we need to address anxiety. But we discover and make use of them only through action. We must let go and move on to make the journey. We will never get "home" if we cling to first, second, or third base.

Support Groups

There are support groups available that address any number of problems. Many of these support groups deal with issues that cause anxiety and worry. Become a part of a support group suited to your needs. You will find that you are not alone. You will get information and insight. Exchanging stories, feelings, and ideas in a structured support system of fellow-sufferers provides companionship that also breaks the pattern of isolation.

Education

We use this term in the broadest possible sense, not just in terms of formal education. Education literally means "to be led out." Learning "leads us out" of the anxiety that chokes off life. Gathering and processing information about anxiety—external and internal—gives us power over our fears. It helps tame runaway imagination and arms the mind to take appropriate action. Knowledge and insight replace speculation and help slow the spinning mind. They inoculate us against our culture's tendency to sell fear through advertising, news stories, television, movies, and simplistic religion. Finally, within the framework of education, exposure to the arts, literature, and music provides a counterbalance to life's ugliness, violence, stupidity, and banality.

Care

Care for our physical bodies helps deal with anxiety. As we have pointed out, anxiety is rooted in the physiology and biology of anxiety. Anxiety is hardwired and produces dis-ease in both body and mind. Attention to taking care of our bodies helps take care of our brains.

1. Exercise

Exercising your body exorcises your brain! Daily exercise does wonders for mental health. In a sense, tell yourself and your worry to "take a hike." When you do, your body releases chemicals that release the intensity of worry. It is not so much an issue of mind over matter, but brain over mind. We feel better and calmer—and know that we do— after exercise.

2. Sleep

We have spoken of the spiritual exercise of disengaging from the domination of the world. This frees us physically and mentally. Sleep is a form of physical and mental disengagement. It prepares us for engaging in physical and mental activity. It also prepares us for emotional engagement. A dictionary definition of sleep is instructive here.

Webster's II New College Dictionary (2005) defines sleep as "a natural, periodically recurring physiological state of rest, characterized by relative physical and nervous inactivity, unconsciousness, and lessened responsiveness to external stimuli." In relationship to worry, we not only need to take a hike, we need to "sleep it off."

Research into sleep and sleep disorders has grown vastly in recent years and provides another tool of dealing with our anxiety and worry connected with our biological nature. We cannot sleep because we are anxious; lack of sleep feeds our anxiety and intensifies worry. Without good sleep in proper amounts, we are exhausted physically and mentally, and we are also restless and irritable. The amount of sleep a person needs varies from individual to individual. But we can begin to determine our own sleep requirements by paying attention to how we feel after differing amounts of sleep. Regular sleep patterns (time to bed and time to rise) are also important. If sleeping problems persist, there are sleep clinics that treat sleep disorders. You should avail yourself of their expertise.

3. Eat Healthy

The effect of diet on physical and mental health is becoming increasingly clear as more research is done. We know that diet contributes to disease—diabetes, heart disease, hypertension, and cancer, to name a few. Too much of anything, even good things, is detrimental to our physical and mental health. Too much sugar, caffeine, nicotine, and alcohol has devastating effects on the body—and the brain is part of the body. Healthy eating begins with eating to live, not living to eat.

Compare and Contrast

The future is filled with both danger and possibility, and we may either succumb to anxiety or we can move ahead to participate in the future. Comparing and contrasting the possible results of our choices and actions is an important tool in dealing with anxiety. They help us establish which values are important to us. They prepare us to confront the unavoidable anxiety that plagues us, no matter what decisions we make. What happens if we give in to anxiety and are paralyzed? (Make a list, if necessary.) By contrast, what happens if we move ahead, even in the face of anxiety? (Consider making another list.) What is to be gained and what is to be lost with each choice? If we see greater gain in moving ahead, we are empowered to release our hold on the present for the sake of the future. We have found the courage to live. This gives us hope.

Continue

We move forward to liberated living by "taking steps." Keep on keeping on is the only remedy for worry. Perseverance—the courage and the will to keep on walking—is powerful. And we are speaking of steps, not leaps and bounds. In an age when, as Woody Allen says, "Instant gratification is not quick enough," we want fast and easy solutions. Dealing with anxiety and worry is a lifelong process, made up of small steps. Small steps move us forward and test our fears.

Choose

A recurrent theme in the Bible is the invitation to "choose life." Yes, we live within certain limitations. Yes, we have parameters that are pre-determined. We fail. We suffer. We are disappointed. Still, there is always an open invitation to choose life. We must school ourselves in the art of making choices. We cannot always choose what happens to us, but we can choose our reactions to circumstances. We are sometimes victims, but we are not *just* victims.

Choosing life—in the face of circumstances—is the art of becoming ourselves before God. It is gift and task, grace and commitment, acceptance and action. It is both faith and works. It is both receiving and giving. It is the courage to be vulnerable in order to choose life and be open to others, open to the future, and open to God. In courage, take the leap of faith. In vulnerability, risk love. In abandonment, practice hope. Remember Kierkegaard's insight: "If we learn to be anxious in the right way, we have learned the most important thing."

WALK ON

The Freedom March as Metaphor

This book has been about freedom. The freedom to live in the midst of anxiety. We believe the freedom marches of the civil rights movement in America serve as a metaphor for understanding what we have been saying about anxiety.

Racism was woven into the social fabric of our culture. Like anxiety, racism was part of daily life. The country was paralyzed. Courageous men, women, and children faced the terrible dilemma: do we give in and give up both freedom and the future, or do we act and take small steps toward freedom and a future? Those who embraced nonviolence chose to take steps toward freedom. Literally, they walked and kept on walking. The few were joined by many, and the walk became a march. They had the courage to take risks. They found their life-task and committed to it. They created community. Those small steps in a life-task, taken in courage and community, took them all the way to freedom.

In actuality, those were anxious times with anxious people. Worry accompanied every moment. Fear stalked every action. Each individual experienced it personally, and together they felt it communally. And they failed. At least partially. Racism has not been eliminated in our society. But it was an incredibly important, successful start, moving ahead with small steps taken with courage, in faith, in love, and in hope. What did they do to accomplish so much?

> **They confronted** their fears, their circumstances, the outer threats, and the inner worries.
>
> **They clarified** by holding teach-ins, planning long-range goals, and by seeking the support of government agencies and the legal system.
>
> **They connected** with each other, with their faith communities, and with their faith source. They worshiped, they sang, they prayed.
>
> **They cared** for each other, for others, for their cause, and the future.
>
> **They compared and contrasted** what would happen if they moved ahead with what would happen if they didn't. What were the benefits and the drawbacks of moving ahead? What would happen if they did nothing?
>
> **They continued** day after day, week after week, year after year. In the midst of failure, in the midst of setback, in the midst of suffering, in the midst of tragedy, they kept on keeping on.
>
> **They chose** life. They chose freedom. They chose to become themselves before God.

And, of course, the march goes on. For racial equality, and for abundant life of every kind. Freedom is always a lifelong march. In the words of the spiritual, "It's a mighty hard climb up to Canaan land." There was much to worry about then: outside threats and internal fears. There was much to win and much to lose, including life itself, and some paid with their lives. But they set in motion an ongoing upward climb for us all. May we be so wise with our own anxiety and worry. March on to freedom! In St. Augustine's words, "Sing Hallelujah! And keep on walking."

SOURCES AND SUGGESTIONS FOR FURTHER READING

Alexander, Bishop, ed. *Selected Lives of the Saints*. As reproduced in Missionary Leaflet number EA01, La Canado, CA: Holy Trinity Orthodox Mission, 2001. See also J. McSorley, "St. Basil the Great," *The Catholic Encyclopedia*. New York: Robert Appleton Company, 1907.

Alves, Rubem. *What Is Religion?* Translated by Don Vinzant. Maryknoll: Orbis Books, 1984.

Auden, W. H. "The Age of Anxiety" in *Collected Poems*. Edited by Edward Mendelson. New York: Random House, 1976.

Barlow, David. *Anxiety and Its Disorders*. New York: Guilford Press, 1988.

Bonhoeffer, Dietrich. *Letters and Papers from Prison*. New Greatly Enlarged Edition. New York: Macmillan, 1972.

Bourne, Edmund, and Lorna Garano. *Coping With Anxiety*. Oakland: New Harbinger, 2003.

Buttrick, George A. *The Parables of Jesus*. New York: Harper and Brothers Publishers, 1928.

Coffin, William Sloane. *The Courage to Love*. San Francisco: Harper and Row, 1982.

Craddock, Fred B., John H. Hayes, Carl R. Holladay, and Gene M. Tucker. *Preaching Through the Christian Year, B*. Valley Forge: Trinity International Press, 1993.

Eliot, T. S. "Choruses from the Rock" and "The Love Song of J. Alfred Prufrock" in *The Complete Poems and Plays*. New York: Harcourt Brace and Co., 1952.

Feuerbach, Ludwig. *The Essence of Christianity*. Translated by George Eliot. New York: Harper, 1957.

Fischer, William F. *Theories of Anxiety*. New York: Harper and Row, 1970.

Frankl, Viktor. *Doctor of the Soul*. New York: Vantage Books, Random House, 1986.

_____. *Man's Search for Meaning*. New York: Simon and Schuster/Touchstone, 1984.

Gerzon, Robert. *Finding Serenity in the Age of Anxiety*. New York: MacMillan, 1997.

Hall, Douglas John. *Professing the Faith*. Minneapolis: Fortress Press, 1993.

Hallowell, Edward M. *Worry: Controlling It and Using It Wisely*. New York: Pantheon Books, 1997.

Hiltner, Seward. *Religion and Health*. New York: MacMillan, 1943.

Hiltner, Seward, and Karl Menninger, eds. *Constructive Aspects of Anxiety*. Nashville: Abingdon Press, 1963.

Hunter, R. Lanny, and Victor L. *What Your Doctor and Your Pastor Want You To Know About Depression*. St. Louis: Chalice Press, 2004.

Kierkegaard, Søren. Edited and Translated by Reidar Thomte in collaboration with Albert B. Anderson. *The Concept of Anxiety*. Princeton: Princeton University Press, 1980.

_____. *The Concept of Dread*. Translated by Walter Lowrie. Princeton: Princeton University Press. 1944.

Kurtz, Ernest, and Katherine Ketcham. *The Spirituality of Imperfection*. New York: Bantam Books, 1992.

Luther, Martin. *Works*. Philadelphia: A. J. Holman and Co. and Castle Press, 1915.

May, Rollo. *The Meaning of Anxiety*. New York: W. W. Norton and Company, 1977.

Moltmann, Jürgen. *Experiences of God*. Translated by Margaret Kohl. Philadelphia: Fortress Press, 1980. See also Jurgen Moltmann, *The Experiment Hope*, edited, translated, and with a foreword by M. Douglas Meeks, Philadelphia: Fortress Press, 1975; and *The Crucified God*, translated by R. A. Wilson and John Bowden, San Francisco: Harper and Row, 1974.

Morris, Robert C. "The Fear of the Lord." *Weavings: A Journal of the Christian Spiritual Life*. Volume XIV, Issue 2 (March/April 1999).

Niebuhr, Reinhold. *The Nature and Destiny of Man*. Vol. 1, Human Nature. Vol. 2, Human Destiny. New York: Scribner, 1964.

Oates, Wayne E. *Anxiety in Christian Experience*. Waco: Word Books, 1955.

Perkins, Robert L., ed. *International Kierkegaard Commentary: The Concept of Anxiety*. Macon: Mercer University Press, 1985.

Phillips, J. B. *Your God Is Too Small*. London: Epworth Press, 1952.

Robinson, John A. T. *The Body: A Study in Pauline Theology*. First published London: SCM Press, 1952. Reprinted Colorado Springs: Bimillennial Press, 2002.

Rogers, Carl. "The Interpersonal Relationship: The Core of Guidance." *Person to Person*. Lafayette, CA: Real People Press, 1967. See also *Client Centered Therapy*, Boston: Houghton Mifflin Company, 1951, and *On Becoming a Person: A Therapist's View of Psychotherapy*, Boston: Houghton Mifflin Company, 1961.

Ross, Jerilyn. *Triumph Over Fear*. New York: Bantam Books, 1994.

Smith, D. Moody. *First, Second and Third John in Interpretation: A Bible Commentary For Teaching and Preaching*. Louisville: John Knox Press, 1991.

Stinnette, Charles R. Jr. *Anxiety and Faith*. Greenwich: Seabury Press, 1955.

Stroup, George. *The Promise of Narrative Theology*. Atlanta: John Knox Press, 1981.

Thomas, Lewis. *The Medusa and the Snail*. New York: Penguin, 1979.

Thornton, Lionel. *The Common Life of the Body of Christ*. London: Dacre Press, 1941.

Tillich, Paul. *The Courage to Be*. 32nd printing. New Haven: Yale University Press, 1969.

_____. "To Whom Much Was Forgiven" in *Parabola*, August 1987.

Wink, Walter. *Transforming Bible Study*. Revised and expanded edition. Nashville: Abingdon Press, 1989.

About the Authors

R. Lanny Hunter is a doctor and author. His specialty is dermatology, and he has practiced since 1971 in northern Arizona. He received his doctorate in medicine from the University of Kansas School of Medicine, interned at Ben Taub General Hospital in Houston, and completed his specialty training at the University of Minnesota. He served as a medical officer in the U.S. Army Special Forces and is a decorated Vietnam veteran. During medical school and his internship, he elected additional training in psychiatry, a special interest of his. He has served on boards and in advisory roles for many organizations, including United Way, the Health Advisory Committee of Northern Arizona University, the Flagstaff Hospice Program, and Flagstaff Medical Center. He lives in Sedona, Arizona.

Victor L. Hunter earned his master of divinity at Union Theological Seminary, specializing in religion and psychiatry, and his doctor of ministry at Phillips Graduate Seminary. He has served as the dean of the Theological Education Institute in Denver, CO, and has taught at Phillips Theological Seminary as adjunct faculty since 1996. He recently retired from working at Evergreen Christian Church in Evergreen, CO, where he had been the pastor since 1985.

He also served for twenty years as retreat director of A Mountain Retreat, a retreat center for ministers dealing with vocational concerns and the stresses of burnout in the ministry. He is now pastoral theologian-at-large for *Table Talk Initiatives*, an emerging coalition of small communities of conversation exploring life and faith in the postmodern world.

The Hunter brothers have collaborated on several writing projects in the past, including *What Your Doctor and Your Pastor Want You to Know about Depression* (Chalice, 2004), and will continue writing together on future projects.